The
FELLOWSHIP
of the
HOLY
SPIRIT

The
FELLOWSHIP
of the
HOLY
SPIRIT

Georgia Harkness

ABINGDON
PRESS
Nashville   New York

THE FELLOWSHIP OF THE HOLY SPIRIT

Copyright © 1966 by Abingdon Press

Library of Congress Catalog Card Number: 66-21188

SET UP, PRINTED, AND BOUND BY THE
PARTHENON PRESS, AT NASHVILLE,
TENNESSEE, UNITED STATES OF AMERICA

TO
MY COLLEAGUES

at Garrett Theological Seminary
and
The Pacific School of Religion

*whose friendship I treasure
as a gift of the Holy Spirit*

ACKNOWLEDGMENTS

I wish to acknowledge gratefully my indebtedness to three friends from the faculty of the Pacific School of Religion, Dr. John Herbert Otwell in Old Testament, Dr. Wilhelm Wuellner in New Testament, and Dr. John von Rohr in Historical Theology and History of Christianity, who have read the chapters in their respective fields. They have given me valuable suggestions, though any remaining errors are mine. I am indebted also to the editorial staff of Abingdon Press, and in particular to my friend and former student Dr. Paul Pettit, for suggestions which have strengthened the book. To my friend and companion Verna Miller I am grateful, as always, not only for her typing of the manuscript but for many other forms of helpfulness.

ACKNOWLEDGMENTS

CONTENTS

9

I

I BELIEVE
IN
THE HOLY SPIRIT

Christians for many centuries and in many languages have affirmed belief in the Holy Spirit. Whether in the traditional English diction, "I believe in the Holy Ghost," or the more contemporary form, "I believe in the Holy Spirit," this affirmation is still made in thousands of services of corporate worship. But do we thus believe? Most Christians would say Yes—and then if pressed would be at a considerable loss to say what this is in which they believe. Holy Ghost or Holy Spirit, the concept is a "ghostly" one to many modern Christians, however implicitly believed or reverently affirmed.

1. WHAT IS THE HOLY SPIRIT?

At first glance there seems no problem, for the Holy Spirit means God—God present with us and within us. God we know and Christ we know, not all about them, but enough for Christian living. But what is this third element in the Trinity? Are not "God the Father Almighty, maker of heaven and earth" and "Jesus Christ, his only Son our Lord" sufficient? Many Christians who think of themselves as Trinitarians are

11

in reality binitarians, though they may not be familiar with the word.

This is no new phenomenon. And the theologians, whether in the formative days of Christian doctrine among the church fathers or subsequently, have been more concerned to affirm and defend the Trinity than to say precisely what is meant by the third element in it. The existence of the Spirit has seldom been questioned. This could hardly be otherwise, for references are found throughout the Bible, from Genesis 1:2 to Revelation 22:17. Two, in particular, include the Holy Spirit in an embryonic statement of the Trinity, "Go therefore and make disciples of all nations, baptizing them in the name of the Father and of the Son and of the Holy Spirit" (Matt. 28:19) and the apostolic benediction with which Paul ends his second letter to the Corinthians, "The grace of the Lord Jesus Christ and the love of God and the fellowship of the Holy Spirit be with you all" (II Cor. 13:14).

Belief in the Holy Spirit has long seemed basic to Christian orthodoxy, whether stated in the one-sentence affirmation of the Apostles' Creed or the more extended and sonorous declaration of the Nicene: "And I believe in the Holy Ghost, the Lord, and Giver of life, who proceedeth from the Father and the Son, who with the Father and the Son together is worshiped and glorified, who spake by the prophets."

Yet the relation of the Holy Spirit to the other aspects of Christian faith and to the life of the Christian has received less attention in a serious examination than has the Christian understanding of God, Christ, man, the church, the kingdom, salvation, eternal life, or any other Christian doctrine. A brief glance at the relative number of books on these themes listed in the card catalog of any theological library will make this evident. Fortunately there has been something of a correction of this trend in recent years.

Nor is this a matter solely of academic interest, or one to be dealt with only in the field of systematic theology by professional theologians. What a Christian believes, or fails to believe, about the Holy Spirit in the ordinary course of human affairs can make a profound difference in his living. To believe that any strong emotional impulse—even if it stems from one's own subconscious desires or from crowd psychology—is the voice of the Holy Spirit can do incalculable harm in fostering neurotic or antisocial behavior. To regard the Holy Spirit simply as a vague something-or-other with a religious aura can deprive the Christian of the divine strength and guidance which the Spirit seeks to impart. Yet, fortunately, this need not be our situation. To believe in the Holy Spirit with a conviction in which sound understanding and personal commitment meet can greatly vivify and enrich human living.

The Holy Spirit means God present with us and God acting for us. To speak of the Holy Spirit is to think of God as intimately near, contemporary with human living in every time and place. The term signifies that "God the Father Almighty, maker of heaven and earth" is also our companion to guide and strengthen us. The older term of the King James Version, "the communion of the Holy Ghost," may not suggest this very adequately. The Revised Standard Version more meaningfully and more accurately translates the third term of the familiar benediction as "the fellowship of the Holy Spirit." This says it exactly, for the supreme gift of the Holy Spirit to any who will receive it is an undergirding fellowship with God.

While other religions affirm belief in a divine Spirit or

many spirits, "the Holy Spirit" is a distinctively Christian term. The Holy Spirit as the living Christ, present with us through all time, continues the work and ministry of Jesus. It is through the Holy Spirit that the love of God and the call to obedience to the will of God, to which Jesus witnessed with his life and death and resurrection, are brought anew to every age.

To put this as succinctly as possible, let me quote two modern affirmations of faith which are widely used in services of worship in Methodist churches. Both are elements in more inclusive statements which affirm in contemporary language the basic tenets of Christian faith.

We believe in the Holy Spirit as the divine presence in our lives, whereby we are kept in perpetual remembrance of the truth of Christ, and find strength and help in time of need.

We believe in the Holy Spirit, God present with us for guidance, for comfort, and for strength.[1]

---

[1] The history of these modern creeds may be of interest to Methodists and others. In *The Methodist Hymnal* and *The Book of Worship* are included, along with the historic affirmations of faith, a modern affirmation and the so-called Korean Creed from which the above citations are taken. No authorship is indicated, for creeds are corporate rather than individual statements of faith. Their history has been given to me by Bishop Herbert E. Welch, who was the principal author of the Korean Creed.

The first of these was written by the late Edwin G. Lewis of Drew Theological School at the request of Bishop W. P. Thirkield, then chairman of the Methodist Episcopal Commission on Worship and Music, who asked Professor Lewis to draft a brief statement of Christian faith which, in addition to the Apostles' Creed, might be commended to the church.

When Bishop Welch was in charge of the Methodist Episcopal churches in Korea, it became apparent that a creedal statement was needed for use in the Orient, with its religious and intellectual history so different from that of the West. In 1930 when the autonomous Korean Methodist Church

We shall come back later to these affirmations to explore their deeper meanings. Yet if what is said in them is true, it becomes immediately apparent that the Holy Spirit is not a theological doctrine only, but is vitally relevant to human need as this is epitomized in man's perennial search for a good, a strong, and a meaningful existence.

2. THE HOLY SPIRIT IN TODAY'S WORLD

But do we need to believe in the Holy Spirit today? In view of the long neglect of this doctrine by theologians and its oversimplification by ordinary Christians, some may contend that it would be better to look elsewhere for our sources of guidance, comfort, and strength. So let us glance in a preliminary way at the difference a genuine belief in the Holy Spirit might make today in the personal experience of Christians, our churches, and our world.

No one needs to be told that these are troubled times. To say nothing of turmoil elsewhere in the world scene, here in America, underneath a veneer of gay lightheartedness such as is apt to accompany a comfortable affluence, there is a great deal of anxiety and unrest. Some of this is evident in the increase of alcoholism, narcotics addiction, sexual perversion and loose sex morals, and many forms of crime. More subtly, it is evidenced in a widespread slipping of moral standards,

---

was about to be formed, the commissioners of the two uniting Methodist Episcopal Churches asked Bishop Welch to prepare a Christian creed that would be couched in simple and nontechnical language. With slight modification this was adopted for use in the Korean Church.

The optional use of both of these creeds was confirmed by the General Conference of the Methodist Episcopal Church and later by the Uniting Conference of 1939 which formed the present Methodist Church.

family instability, and an increase in emotional disturbances which send persons to the psychiatrist if one can pay the fees and to the pastoral counselor if one cannot. Add to these factors racial tension, outbreaks of rioting and violence, extremism of the left and of the right, and the ugly realities of war, and it becomes clear that the situation in human affairs is far from good.

Such developments accent, under changing conditions, perennial human tendencies. The changes are due to a complex network of social factors which it would be extraneous at this point to enumerate. The changes taking place in our society are by no means all bad. Some are very good, and significant elements of progress as well as retrogression are discernible.[2] What is relevant to our present concern is the fact that underneath the changing social fabric lie unchanging human needs. Though manifold in their complexity they center in the need to have faith instead of fear, hope instead of despair, love instead of self-seeking and the inner loneliness that so often accompanies it. It was with profound insight that Paul wrote, "So faith, hope, love abide, these three; but the greatest of these is love."

The Christian need not doubt that these three by the sustaining power of God will abide to the end of time, and will abide not only as a quest but in some measure as an achievement. Yet this is not to say that they do abide in every individual, and even the best of Christians must battle to maintain them. When the implicit and often unrealized demand of the human spirit for faith, hope, and love is not

[2] I have canvassed these factors at some length in *Our Christian Hope*, (Abingdon, 1964), Chap. III, which is entitled "Can We Believe in Progress?"

met, aberrations occur not only in the personal experience of individuals but corporately in great social groups. When these needs are ministered to and met even partially, but with the assurance that life has meaning and richness because of them, victorious and stable living becomes possible. Though life remains precarious and there is no guarantee of untroubled living for anybody, life's vicissitudes can then be confronted with courage, serenity, and a sense of direction.

It is not in Christianity alone that foundations of faith, hope, and love are found. Secular society prizes these values also, and other faiths have their varied approaches to the good life. Wherever faith, hope, and love, or to cite another familiar trilogy, goodness, truth, and beauty, are found Christians ought to rejoice instead of claiming these values as the exclusive terrain of Christians. Yet it still remains true, verified by the empirical evidence of the centuries, that no other faith or mode of approach to life has done so much to lift, ennoble, purify, and strengthen human life as has the gospel of Jesus Christ. This remains true in spite of the fact that it has always been channeled through imperfect human instruments.

What has this to do with the Holy Spirit? Christians believe that it is not the imperfect human instruments alone, but the power of God working through them and even at times in spite of them, that has brought about this fruitage and continues to do so. If it is the Holy Spirit that mediates to us the gospel of Jesus Christ, whether through the Church, the Bible, the lives and works of Christians, or any other agency, then it is imperative that we listen obediently and intelligently to the Spirit's leading.

To return to the ills mentioned above, let it be stated as

emphatically as possible that the Holy Spirit is not to be regarded as a cure-all! A peace of mind that acquiesces in
evil is dearly bought, and in the end self-defeating. Christian
faith must be integrated with the totality of life, and when
"the spiritual life" is dissociated from the material, political,
cultural, and other basic factors in human existence, it becomes an extraneous luxury and a perversion of the Christian
gospel rather than a true channel of the Holy Spirit.

This perversion is apt to be present in some degree in every
church, and in those churches which profess to preach and
teach only in the field of spiritual matters the imperatives of
Christian faith are dangerously circumscribed. This appears
to be the main reason for the current emphasis on "religionless Christianity," with its new modes of outreach to the
secular world and an emphasis on the need to carry the ethical demands of Jesus out from the sanctuary and into the
world. At this point clear distinctions must be drawn. With
any useful service to humanity in the name and spirit of
Jesus, fellow Christians ought to be sympathetic and as far as
possible cooperative. However, this does not call for agreement with all the moods and movements that have emerged
in recent years. Some are constructive, others questionable.
In fact, since they move in such varying directions, one could
hardly agree with them all.

Religionless Christianity in my judgment is a contradiction
in terms, and because of its illogicality it is a meaningless
term. There could be Christianity without denominations.
We are not apt to do away rapidly with those we have, but in
the early days of the Christian fellowship there were none.
No form of institutional structure is sacrosanct. The Church
of Christ has shown itself able to survive many cultural

and internal changes within the successive periods of history, and doubtless will continue to do so. What the Church could not survive, were it to occur on an extensive scale, would be the loss of that element of religion which centers in faith in the living God revealed in Jesus Christ. This is not all there is of the Christian religion, but it stands at its most pivotal and focal point.

What this means in relation to the Holy Spirit is twofold. From the objective side, the sustaining power and presence of the God revealed in Jesus may be counted on to continue in the world, whatever the shifts in human events and ideologies. He is present in both mercy and judgment regardless of the degree to which his presence is acknowledged, and declaring the demise of God will not eliminate him from the human scene. Yet from the subjective angle, our response in obedience and trust to the Holy Spirit's leading is imperative if Christian faith is to be vital and relevant in each new era. God works through human instruments, and the response of Christ's followers to the Spirit's presence "for guidance, for comfort, and for strength" is a basic need.

There are evidences about us today of what might be termed—paraphrasing a familiar term in biblical scholarship —"a new quest of the Holy Spirit." Reference has been made to the increased publication of books in this field. In the area of worship, this has its counterpart in the liturgical movement and the enrichment of worship through both new and traditional forms of adoration, praise, and petition. There is a comparable movement in spiritual retreats for laymen and emphasis on the personal devotional life through the meeting of small groups for spiritual examination and growth. This is apparently not the day of great mystical literature, but much useful writing is being done through books, periodicals, and devotional manuals to enrich the life of personal fellowship with God.

Not everything that is being done in this area is fully commendable or Christian. As indicated earlier, some of it is too self-centered and remote from the obligation to help fashion a better world. There are contemporary far-out movements such as yoga, reincarnation, karma, Zen, psychedelics, and spiritualism, to say nothing of a multitude of metaphysical cults, which the Christian does well to learn about but not to embrace.

There are disputed issues, such as spiritual healing and glossolalia, or the speaking in tongues, which have recently moved from the "holiness" sects into some of the "old line" churches. Whether such movements are to be judged favorably or repudiated hinges mainly on one's understanding of the work of the Holy Spirit in relation to other factors in human existence.

In addition to such movements as those mentioned which bear an obvious relation to the Holy Spirit are many others. The Christian may well believe that the Holy Spirit is at work in the ecumenical movement, and perhaps in particular that aspect of it in which Roman Catholic and Protestant Christians are drawing closer together in mutual understanding and fellowship. There is evidence of the Spirit's presence in the newer understanding of mission in the Church as the calling of every Christian to service within his particular vocation and circumstances, and in the awakening response of the Church both as a visible institution and as a latent force to the demand for freedom and justice in a revolutionary age.

These movements are unmistakably present. Some of them are centrally, others only tangentially, related to historic Christianity. Have they in fact come into being through the work of the Holy Spirit? And to what extent are they responsive to the Spirit's leading? Or do they perhaps represent a replacement of this leading with human wisdom or even with human presumption?

These are important questions. Yet they are questions not easily answered. Persons committed to these movements, provided their thinking is still within the framework of the Christian tradition, will in most cases see in them some signs of the Holy Spirit's leading. Those opposed will say that this is a false claim, and perhaps even a blatant attempt to hallow and deify a mistaken human impulse. Those who have broken with historic Christianity or have never stood within it are prone to dismiss the whole idea of the Holy Spirit as wishful thinking and the product of human imagination.

3. A PREVIEW OF PROCEDURE

It is not the purpose of this book to give an extended treatment of such movements or to try to answer all the questions that can be raised about them. Rather, its aim is to give some groundwork for an answer to both the theological and practical problems that arise in connection with belief in the Holy Spirit.

Since belief in the Spirit of God was an element in religious experience long before it became the doctrine of the Holy Spirit, we must begin with the historical backgrounds. This calls for a chapter to examine its place in Old Testament thought. Two chapters then explore what we find in the

21

New Testament. One of these chapters deals with the point of view of the first three Gospels and with that crucial event in the birth of the Church, the coming of the Holy Spirit at Pentecost. The other examines what the Spirit meant to the nascent Church as this is reflected in Acts, the letters of Paul, and the Fourth Gospel.

Since the Holy Spirit as doctrine gets its justification and validity from the Holy Spirit in experience, a transitional chapter from biblical to theological perspectives seems next to be required. The primary notes in the work of the Holy Spirit are traced in a chapter which carries forward the biblical foundations while relating them also to the permanent human situation.

The sixth, seventh, and eighth chapters are primarily theological, for they aim to relate belief in the Holy Spirit to the doctrine of the Trinity, to the Church in its various phases and forms of ecclesiology, and to the human spirit. In the chapter on biblical and contemporary views of human nature an attempt is made to provide some criteria for answering a perennial question, "How do we know when it is the Holy Spirit that speaks, and not our own sinful and distorted human impulses claiming divine authority?"

The ninth chapter has a twofold purpose. It aims to state the author's judgment on some issues in regard to the Holy Spirit on which there is no general agreement among Christians. This is followed by a setting forth of certain central guidelines for action by the Spirit's leading in matters of difficult ethical decision with some suggestions as to how these guidelines may be applied in a concrete contemporary issue.

The final chapter deals with the Holy Spirit in the life of

today, and it picks up for further consideration some of the issues mentioned in this introductory survey. While the scope of the book is for the most part biblical and theological analysis, it is hoped that the relevance of the Holy Spirit to Christian living will at no point be lost sight of by either the author or the reader.

The Holy Spirit is God with us and God for us, and this to the Christian means "the Divine Presence in our lives, whereby we are kept in perpetual remembrance of the truth of Christ, and find strength and help in time of need." Amid the conditions of our confused world wherein many discordant voices are heard and human wisdom often seems inadequate, is anything else more needed?

II

THE SPIRIT
IN
THE OLD TESTAMENT

The preliminary look at the Holy Spirit presented in the previous chapter must be greatly expanded. Yet if the reader will hold in mind these outlines, it may facilitate understanding as we search amid the varying nuances of both biblical and theological thought to find further meaning for the term.

Our first major task must now be the examination of the biblical basis for belief in the Holy Spirit. While the Spirit does not appear as a doctrine in the Old Testament, and not always as "holy" either in name or nature, we shall not understand its presence either in the New Testament or later without a look at its roots.

For these roots, we must go back beyond the Old Testament into the characteristic patterns of primitive religion. This need not alarm us if we are careful not to commit the fallacy of supposing that the higher forms of religious belief and practice can all be explained by origins, or that these origins "explain away" the reality or the significance of divine activity. Christian faith as it centers in the revelation and redemptive power of God in Jesus Christ is not discredited by the fact that other religions, and even primitive ones, have sought knowledge of the divine and salvation from life's evils by channels that are different, yet not wholly different, from the Christian way.

Nor need we be surprised to find that there are differing views of the Holy Spirit within the Bible. A basic requirement for understanding the Bible's basic meaning and message is the recognition that differing historical situations and social conditions, as well as differences of personality and purpose, are reflected in the words of its many authors. The Bible is still the Word of God, for he speaks through the Bible as through no other book. Yet it has become a commonplace of biblical scholarship that the Bible reflects a rich diversity within which there are elements that cannot be fully synthesized, and in which there are changing and for the most part growing insights. This will be noted repeatedly as we look at what the Bible says about the Holy Spirit.

1. THE ROOTS IN PRIMITIVE THOUGHT

A brief, preliminary look at the Old Testament will give groundwork for noting what was taken over from primitive thought and transformed in the taking. It is equally a mistake to deny the presence of primitive ideas and practices in the Old Testament or to identify these with its major message.

The word most often used in the Old Testament to denote "spirit" is *ruach*, which means "wind" or "breath." *Ruach* came also to mean "life" or "the spirit of life" because breath is so essential to life. This combination of ideas was taken over into the Greek *pneuma* and the Latin *anima* and *spiritus*.

Thus *ruach* in the Old Testament applies both to the Spirit of God and to the human spirit, though for the latter the word *nephesh*, usually translated "soul," is more often used.

The *ruach* of God was not identical with his total being, but was a power, or principle of being, that could be sent forth to act either upon the inanimate world or upon humans. Thus "the Lord God formed man of dust from the ground, and breathed into his nostrils the breath of life; and man became a living being" (Gen. 2:7). In a much later account of creation, though it stands earlier and is the magnificent hymn with which the Bible opens, we find the words, "The earth was without form and void, and darkness was upon the face of the deep; and the Spirit of God was moving over the face of the waters" (Gen. 1:2).[1] The importance of this passage in reference to the cosmos we shall note later. However, it was chiefly upon individuals that God (Jahweh) bestowed his Spirit. Repeatedly we find examples of how the *ruach* of God gave to individual persons superhuman powers that they would not otherwise have had.

The word for "holy" in the Hebrew is *qodesh*. Though the old Testament has much to say of the holiness of God, the words *ruach* and *qodesh* are found in combination only in two passages, Psalm 51:11 and Isaiah 63:10, 11. In the first of these, the familiar

> Cast me not away from thy presence,
> and take not thy holy Spirit from me,

---

[1] Since the word used here for "move" connotes elsewhere "to hover over" or "to brood," what is suggested is a divine, vitalizing energy. The Moffatt translation reads, "When God began to form the universe, the world was void and vacant, darkness lay over the abyss; but the spirit of God was hovering over the waters."

"thy holy Spirit" is the equivalent of "thy presence" in the repetitional parallelism of Hebrew poetry, and this may be true of the second though the connection is less clear. Both passages suggest the nearness of the divine Spirit, while the many references to the divine holiness in the Old Testament suggest the majesty of God and the reverent awe with which men should regard him.

The significance of this for later thought lies in the fact that in *ruach* and *qodesh* are already found intimations of what the Holy Spirit was to come to mean—God acting and God present, yet not with a nearness that could be trifled with. It was as the Spirit of God, mysterious and powerful, came upon persons or the world that mighty things were done.

Yet how is this related to origins? Something of a similar nature appears quite commonly in primitive religions, whether of the past or in primitive cultures of the present.

As is well known, primitive religion is animistic, with a multitude of spirits both good and evil inhabiting not only human and animal bodies but what we regard as inanimate things. Not all of these spirits were gods, but the more important such as the sun-god or moon-god or the deity that gave fertility to the fields or flocks were so regarded. These gods and spirits did whatever man in his ordinary powers could not do. Not only did they create the world: they sent the rain to water it, gave it fertility, stirred the sea with mighty storms, caused the volcano to belch forth lava and rivers to flow in torrents over waterfalls. They gave success to the hunter and to the armies in battle. On their help everything most important in life depended; hence, the need of magical incantations and sacrificial offerings to propitiate their anger and secure their favor.

There is an implicit polytheism in this which became explicit in Greek and Roman thought. Yet there is also an implicit monism—a movement away from a multitude of spirits to Spirit. This was not so much a later development as an inherent aspect of animism, for the spirits had their efficacy from the possession of a pervasive undifferentiated power. The anthropologists call this power "mana," from the terminology of the Melanesians, but the belief in its existence is found in virtually all primitive cultures. It is the source of the hunter's or the warrior's skill, the field's fertility, and of everything else that matters.

2. OLD TESTAMENT ADAPTATIONS

The early Hebrews, like other early cultures, had a belief in divinity that dwelt in trees, springs, wells, stones, and mountains. This caused them to regard such places as sacred. The Old Testament abounds in illustrations,[2] though the blending of primitivism with the worship of Jahweh tends both to obscure and to supersede the primitive elements.

To cite a few examples, there was the sacred oak at Shechem, where Abraham received a divine message (Gen. 12:6), where Jacob hid the foreign gods, presumably to let their power be nullified by a more powerful divinity (Gen. 35:4), where Joshua set up a great stone to witness that it had heard the words of the Lord (Josh. 24:26-27), where Abimelech was made king (Judg. 9:6). Sacred waters, whether wells, springs, or flowing streams, had a particular

[2] The illustrations I have given are taken from Elmer W. K. Mould's *Essentials of Bible History* (Rev. ed.; New York: Ronald Press, 1951), pp. 122-25. He cites some forty biblical references to such sacred places.

significance in a barren land as the abiding place of life-giving deity, and most if not all of the place names beginning with *En* (spring) are believed to have originally been sacred places. Of all the sacred mountains Mt. Sinai was, of course, foremost in Hebrew thought but other mountains sacred to foreign deities before they entered Hebrew history were Mt. Nebo, Mt. Peor, and Mt. Pisgah, all of these being in Moab, and Mt. Carmel and Mt. Zion in the Promised Land.

Many if not most of these sacred places had been so regarded long before the Hebrews entered Canaan, and it would be easy to infer from this that they simply took over what they found. This, however, oversimplifies the situation. While the early Hebrews believed in the presence of divinity in these places, and thus came to regard them as holy, this did not lead them into polytheism. Early Hebrew thought was henotheistic, believing in the existence of the gods of the surrounding nations but rejecting the worship of these gods except in sporadic lapses into apostasy. Exalting the worship of their own God Jahweh, they never developed a pantheon of deities from the personification of natural or social forces. In relation to the sacred places, they were saved both from the cruder forms of animism and from polytheism by not imputing to each a separate spirit, but instead a pervasive Spirit that could be identified with the power and presence of Jahweh.

It is apparent that there are affinities here with the concept of *mana*. This becomes still more evident when it is noted that in early Old Testament literature it is the Spirit's power, rather than moral qualities, that is stressed. All acts which seemed extraordinary were attributed to the Spirit of the Lord. The Spirit comes upon Samson and he tears a lion

29

to pieces with his bare hands (Judg. 14:6); he kills thirty men in Ashkelon and takes their spoil (Judg. 14:19); he snaps the ropes with which he is bound and slays a thousand men with the jawbone of an ass (Judg. 15:14, 15). The Spirit could also prompt one to ecstatic utterance, and upon occasion could be the source of evil as well as good. Thus, the Spirit "came mightily" upon Saul and he prophesied among a traveling band of prophets (I Sam. 10:10); yet after he had risen to power "the Spirit of the Lord departed from Saul, and an evil spirit from the Lord tormented him" (I Sam. 16:14).

3. NEW NOTES

Had the Spirit remained simply the source of extraordinary power, whether physical or psychic, it would have had more in common with primitive religion than with Christian faith. Yet the idea of a divine *ruach*, more than man yet coming upon man through the personal will of the Most High God, had entered Hebrew thinking. We must see now how this took on the attributes of righteousness and holiness.

It was in the great prophets of the eighth through the sixth centuries that the Spirit came to be thought of as endued with the *righteousness* of God. The Spirit, indeed, imparted to men a power that was more than human, as in Zechariah's word, "Not by might, nor by power, but by my Spirit, says the Lord of hosts" (Zech. 4:6). However, this was no longer a power that came upon men like a breath of wind and caused them to do extraordinary and even fantastic things; it was a moral energy that was linked with a vitalizing faith and a call to obedience to the holy and righteous will of God. This is nowhere better illustrated than in the words of Second

Isaiah which Jesus took as his Scripture reading when he preached his first sermon in the Nazareth synagogue:

> The Spirit of the Lord God is upon me,
>   because the Lord has anointed me
> to bring good tidings to the afflicted;
>   he has sent me to bind up the brokenhearted,
> to proclaim liberty to the captives,
>   and the opening of the prison to those who are
>   bound;
> to proclaim the year of the Lord's favor.
>
> (Isa. 61:1, 2; cf. Luke 4:18, 19.)

In such passages the word "Spirit" is capitalized to indicate a moral energy going forth from Jahweh to challenge and animate his people. In others, however, a distinction is drawn by the translators where the word *ruach* is printed "spirit" to indicate an aspect of the nature of Jahweh himself. Since there are no capitals in Hebrew, this difference which is a narrow but important one has to be judged by the context. We find an example in Isaiah 30:1:

> "Woe to the rebellious children," says the Lord,
>   "who carry out a plan, but not mine;
> and who make a league, but not of my spirit,
>   that they may add sin."

Another example which illustrates the use of *ruach* both for the human spirit and the divine spirit is found in Ezekiel 36:26, 27, "A new heart I will give you, and a new spirit I will put within you; and I will take out of your flesh the heart of stone and give you a heart of flesh. And I will put my spirit within you, and cause you to walk in my statutes and be careful to observe my ordinances." We find foreshadowed here a problem still with us in regard to the Holy Spirit—whether this is to be thought of as God himself or as the gift of God—and the answer appears to be that the Spirit is *both*.

Yet while it is the prophets who bring the Hebrew understanding of the Spirit of God to its highest level of moral insight, an apparent paradox confronts us. Three of the prophets of greatest ethical sensitivity, Amos, Hosea and Jeremiah, do not mention the Spirit, and there is but one reference in Micah (3:8). Instead, they assert that their authority comes directly from God in "thus saith the Lord," or "the word of the Lord that came to" one after another of them.

An explanation commonly given is that the erratic and ecstatic utterances of earlier false prophets, who claimed to speak by the Spirit of the Lord, had made these men wary of claiming this ground for the truth of their message. In view of the bizarre distortions today of the authority of the Holy Spirit, this is plausible. It is perhaps supported by the word of Hosea in 9:7,

> The prophet is a fool,
> the man of the spirit is mad,
> because of your great iniquity
> and great hatred.

However, the correct interpretation of this message is more likely to be that the people in their opposition have discredited the prophet's message by calling him crazy, which is again a situation all too common in today's world.

A second type of explanation, which supplements rather

than contradicts the first, is that the "word" of God as revelation of the divine will and purpose was so closely associated with *ruach* that the terms could be used interchangeably. Since in the Old Testament "the word of the Lord" is a term used repeatedly to designate either creation or revelation, and to utter a word is to send forth breath, the identification was a natural one. For example, we find in the thirty-third Psalm:

> By the word of the Lord the heavens were made,
> and all their host by the breath of his mouth. . . .
>
> For he spoke, and it came to be;
> he commanded, and it stood forth. (Vss. 6, 9.)

There are numerous references to *ruach* in Ezekiel which suggest divine control through both the words and acts of the Spirit. (Ezek. 3:24; 8:3; 11:1, 5, 24; 43:5.) For example, "And he said to me, 'Son of man, stand upon your feet, and I will speak with you.' And when he spoke to me, the Spirit entered into me and set me upon my feet; and I heard him speaking to me" (Ezek. 2:1, 2). Repeatedly we find the words, "The Spirit lifted me up." A Christian understanding of the Holy Spirit as both the voice of God and the energizing power of God is thus unconsciously foreshadowed.

Whether as divine direction and power through speech or action, the prophetic conception of the Spirit's work is thoroughly ethical. Righteousness is its undergirding note. This conception, carried over into New Testament thought, later to be incorporated into the main stream of Christian faith, was of tremendous significance.

A further development, characteristic of the Old Testament

but now brought to sharper focus in prophetic thought, is the insight that the work of the Spirit is not only upon individuals but may be *corporate*. This emphasis we find in Ezekiel, Second Isaiah and Joel.

In Ezekiel, the revivifying of the valley of dry bones is a striking picture of what could yet be Israel's destiny (Ezek. 37:1-14). The hand of the Lord was upon the prophet, and by the Spirit of the Lord he was brought to the valley and told to prophesy. After the bones have taken on flesh and begun to breathe again, the Lord God gives the promise:

And you shall know that I am the Lord, when I open your graves, and raise you from your graves, O my people. And I will put my Spirit within you, and you shall live, and I will place you in your own land; then you shall know that I, the Lord, have spoken, and I have done it, says the Lord. (Ezek. 37:13, 14.)

It is clear that this is Jahweh's word of encouragement and hope to exiled Israel. What is not so clear is whether any distinction is to be drawn between the Lord God himself and the Spirit as the breath of life, the promised source of invigoration. The writer apparently did not raise this question, for as yet there was no Trinitarian formula to require strict definition.

In Second Isaiah accent is given to the conviction that the Spirit has led Israel gloriously in the past. So, too, the promise reaches into the future.

> For I will pour water on the thirsty land,
>   and streams on the dry ground;
> I will pour my Spirit upon your descendants,
>   and my blessing on your offspring. (Isa. 44:3.)

Here we find much the same note of revivification as in Ezekiel's vision, though the metaphor is shifted from the reviving of dead bodies to the refreshing of dry land.

The passage in Joel is a familiar one because Peter chose to quote it in his great sermon when the Holy Spirit came upon the waiting disciples at Pentecost. Note that it continues the metaphor of outpouring.

> And it shall come to pass afterward,
>   that I will pour out my spirit on all flesh;
> your sons and your daughters shall prophesy,
>   your old men shall dream dreams,
>   and your young men shall see visions.
> Even upon the menservants and maidservants
>   in those days, I will pour out my spirit.
>   (Joel 2:28, 29; cf. Acts 2:17, 18.)

In all three of these passages which indicate the prophets' conception of the Spirit's revivifying power upon the people corporately, there is an *eschatological* note. However, it is an eschatology of Israel's earthly future. Whether the promise is extended beyond the bounds of Israel to other nations is less clear, but at least in Second Isaiah the context suggests this. Joel's "all flesh" looks in this direction, but is immediately qualified by the statement that it is "your" sons and daughters who are to receive the Spirit.[3] His contribution is the opening of the Spirit equally to male and female, old and

[3] Cf. *The Interpreter's Bible*, vol. 6, pp. 752 f., where the exegesis by John A. Thompson asserts this limitation and calls attention to Peter's extension of the scope of the prophecy to non-Israelite believers. The national exclusiveness found elsewhere in Joel, especially in chap. 3, supports this interpretation.

young, master and servant, and this is of more than a little significance in the movement toward a New Testament outlook.

At the same time that the prophets were moving away from a nonmoral understanding of the Spirit as the source of the extraordinary acts of individuals to a more ethical, corporate, forward-looking and hope-inspiring view, another change was taking place. For this we turn mainly to the psalms.

In the psalms, the devotional poetry that became the hymn-book of the second Temple but which voices the worship and aspiration of many centuries, the emphasis is again on the presence of the Spirit in the life of the individual. This is important for a number of reasons. First, the references are infrequent, the individual's aspiration and assurance being for the most part directly toward and from "the Lord." Second, in the few but great passages where the Spirit is mentioned, what is stressed is the ministry of the Spirit to what has come to be called "the spiritual life." I use this ambiguous phrase somewhat reluctantly for lack of a better one.[4] Its meaning is best discerned from the psalms themselves. As men felt themselves beset with sin, sorrow, loneliness, death, or any of the other of life's baffling mysteries, it was assurance of God's sustaining power and presence that brought comfort and strength. It is for this reason that the book of Psalms is today the most familiar and beloved book of the Old Testament.

With reference to the Spirit, it is not only the goodness but the *omnipresence* of the Spirit that is brought into high

---

[4] The terms "mystical" or "devotional" are often used. However, they are equally ambiguous and open to misinterpretation.

perspective. In Psalm 139 is found what Henry P. Van Dusen calls "the mountain-summit of pre-Christian faith." [5]

> Whither shall I go from thy Spirit?
> Or whither shall I flee from thy presence?
> If I ascend to heaven, thou art there!
> If I make my bed in Sheol, thou art there!
> If I take the wings of the morning
>   and dwell in the uttermost parts of the sea,
> even there thy hand shall lead me,
>   and thy right hand shall hold me. (Ps. 139:7-10.)

The same note is sounded but with the additional note of man's perennial quest for cleansing from sin in Psalm 51, which as already noted is one of the only two passages in the Old Testament where the adjective "holy" is used with Spirit:

> Create in me a clean heart, O God,
>   and put a new and right spirit within me.
> Cast me not away from thy presence,
>   and take not thy holy Spirit from me.
> Restore to me the joy of thy salvation,
>   and uphold me with a willing spirit.
>   (Ps. 51:10-12.)

These passages are significant, not only for deep insight which leads them to be quoted so frequently, but for the fact that they stress the *continuing* rather than the intermittent presence of the Spirit. Does the Spirit come as a divine invasion, an intervention in the ordinary course of human ex-

[5] *Spirit, Son and Father* (New York: Charles Scribner's Sons, 1958), p. 45.

istence? Or is the Spirit always with us if we but open our eyes to see and our ears to hear? Both views are found in the Bible and are found in both the Old Testament and the New. This question goes to the depths of Christian theology, and I shall not attempt to answer it at this point except to say that the two views are not so self-contradictory as they may seem. We shall encounter it again.

Still another development must now be looked at, the reference of the Spirit to the *cosmos*. To this point the examples cited have had to do with the Spirit's work in the lives of persons, whether as individuals or groups. In the earlier literature of the Old Testament, the Spirit is almost never related to the physical universe. This is perhaps due to the general lack of cosmological speculation among the Hebrews. Yet in the later writing a beginning of this interest is seen. The most obvious passage is in the post-exilic account of creation in Genesis 1:2, where the Spirit broods over the waters and brings order out of primordial chaos. It is implied though not expressly stated in Job as the voice from the whirlwind speaks of the marvels of creation and the wisdom of the Almighty in contrast with man's ignorance and weakness (Job 38:1–39:30). A passage in Job often quoted from the King James Version, "By his spirit he hath garnished the heavens" (Job 26:13), becomes in the Revised Standard, "By his wind the heavens were made fair." However, the marvelous nature poetry of Psalm 104 not only implies but states that creation is the work of the divine *ruach*.[6]

---

[6] The alternative rendering is "breath." The Moffatt translation puts it thus: "Yet a breath from thee brings them into being, renewing the face of the earth."

> When thou sendest forth thy Spirit, they are created;
> and thou renewest the face of the ground. (Ps. 104:30.)

Furthermore, along with this conception of the Spirit as brooding over and bringing order into the cosmos, another development of much significance was taking place. This was the belief that *man* in his essential nature was also *ruach*. As in early Hebrew thought man was created through the inbreathing of the breath of life (Gen. 2:7), so in later writing this breath-soul became spirit akin to the divine Spirit. The creation of man in the divine image (Gen. 1:27) reflects this relation although it does not specifically state it. The Hebrews did not have the dualism of flesh and spirit, or the trichotomy of body, mind, and spirit, which developed in later Christian thought. Nevertheless, *ruach* as an aspect of human nature suggested both kinship and channel of communication with the *ruach* of God.[7]

References to the spirit of man appear repeatedly in Job, Proverbs, and Ecclesiastes, though usually without a stated connection with the Spirit of God. However, the relation becomes explicit in such passages as,

> The spirit of man is the lamp of the Lord,
> searching all his innermost parts. (Prov. 20:27.)

In Job 27:1-6 and 33:1-4 the speaker (first Job and then Elihu) ascribes both his existence and his integrity to the spirit of God.

The Bible is unequivocal in regarding God as the Creator

[7] See H. Wheeler Robinson, *The Christian Experience of the Holy Spirit* (New York: Harper & Brothers, 1928), pp. 12 f. for a fuller treatment of this relationship. I deal with it further in chap. VIII.

of nature and of man. Yet, that he created through the Spirit was not fully developed. The doctrine of the Spirit as the creative and ordering principle was merged in the doctrine of the Logos as the Hebrew came in contact with the Greek mind, and we find the fruit of this blending in John 1:1-5.

It remains now to speak of that aspect of the Spirit in the Old Testament which most directly was a preparation for the New; namely, the relation of the Spirit to *the promised Messiah*. Here, again, the references are not numerous but are highly significant. In Isaiah 11 we read:

> And the Spirit of the Lord shall rest upon him,
>> the spirit of wisdom and understanding,
>> the spirit of counsel and might,
>> the spirit of knowledge and the fear of the Lord.
>>> (Isa. 11:2, 3.)

The prophecy then rises to a great crescendo in the words:

> They shall not hurt or destroy
>> in all my holy mountain;
> for the earth shall be full of the knowledge of the Lord
>> as the waters cover the sea. (Isa. 11:9.)

A similar note is expressed in Isaiah 42, although here it is the "servant" who is thus endowed and "spirit" in lower case suggests a divine attribute:

> Behold my servant, whom I uphold,
>> my chosen, in whom my soul delights;
> I have put my spirit upon him,
>> he will bring forth justice to the nations. (Isa. 42:1.)

These notes of a Spirit-imparted wisdom, power, justice, and love all converge in the Servant's acceptance of his commission at the Spirit's call in the words which Jesus quoted as the keynote of his ministry. We have already cited the portion that Luke records, but the remainder of the passage must not be overlooked because it reflects so much not only of a divine imperative in the pursuit of justice but of tender compassion:

> The Spirit of the Lord God is upon me,
>   because the Lord has anointed me
> to bring good tidings to the afflicted; . . .
>   to comfort all who mourn;
> to grant to those who mourn in Zion—
>   to give them a garland instead of ashes,
> the oil of gladness instead of mourning,
>   the mantle of praise instead of a faint spirit;
> that they may be called oaks of righteousness,
>   the planting of the Lord, that he may be glorified.
>   (Isa. 61:1-3.)

Jesus knew his Old Testament Scriptures, and could have read for the lesson in the Nazareth synagogue on that historic morning any one of innumerable other passages. That he chose this one is clear evidence of how he appraised it. We too do well to regard it as the high-water mark of Old Testament insight as to the nature and work of the Spirit of the Lord.

III

THE COMING
OF
THE HOLY SPIRIT

The title of this chapter has intentionally a
double meaning. What it suggests most obviously is Pentecost,
at which we shall be looking before the chapter concludes.
However, a second meaning commonly overlooked inheres
in the fact that "Spirit" as we have seen it in the Old Testament comes in the New Testament to mean "Holy Spirit."
This did not happen all at once, and there was never a sharp
transition in meaning, the term "Spirit" being retained
throughout the New Testament and in the Church to the
present. Yet in the New Testament, certain important
changes took place with the result that today we have a Christian, but not a Jewish, doctrine of the Trinity. It will be our
task in this chapter and the next to trace these changes and
the stages by which they came about.

1. THE TRANSITION

Let us begin by summing up the results of our study thus
far. Although the term "Holy Spirit" as two words with one
meaning is not found in the Old Testament, we have noted

numerous elements that were preparatory to the New Testament understanding and use of the term.

At first a wind-like energy suffused with divinity in a manner not unlike the *mana* of primitive religion was believed to be the source of extraordinary powers. These powers were manifest in the possession by individuals of both superhuman physical strength and ecstatic utterance regarded as "prophesying." In the greater prophets the Spirit was conceived as possessing and imparting moral power, and at the same time was largely identified with "the word of the Lord" as the source of divine inspiration. The Spirit's activity was thought of as directed not only to particular individuals but to Israel as a nation, and in this context the revivifying of Israel through the outpouring of God's Spirit was the central note. In the psalms and other post-exile literature the Spirit speaks to man's inner life to give to the receptive person a quickening and supporting sense of the divine presence and power within the varied conditions of his existence. During the same period the Spirit is thought of also as brooding over and bringing order to the cosmos. In passages that are not the latest in the Old Testament, but are among those of greatest insight, the Spirit is linked with the Messianic hope of a coming Redeemer in whom wisdom, power, justice, and love are united.

a. *The intertestamental period.* There is no need to trace in detail the understanding of the Spirit in the period between the Old and New Testaments. Yet some developments were taking place which foreshadow later stages.

In rabbinic Judaism tendencies were at work which, though seeming to move in different directions, were destined to converge and to cast long shadows into the future. Its conception of the Spirit was, and in another sense was not, ethically oriented. The increased emphasis on the law and on the minutiae of regulations, particularly in regard to the Sabbath, tended to accent a different idea of holiness from that of prophetic moral urgency or mystical Presence. At the same time belief in the infallibility of Scripture, with the Spirit appealed to as its validation, was emerging. "All the writings in the Old Testament are inspired by the Spirit, and the question whether a particular writing should be taken into the Canon is identical with the question whether it was written in the Holy Spirit." [1] Yet the Spirit's inspiration of the Scriptures as a whole did not prevent the attributing of passages to different speakers with the Spirit as one of them, and much ingenuity was exercised to make this distinction. It is apparent that a trend was being inaugurated of which we have not yet seen the last.

Yet along with such legalism and potential biblical literalism, rabbinic thought had also a strong sense of the relation of the Spirit to a devout and God-fearing life. And if the passages which look in this direction are probed, it will be seen that the Spirit which makes for righteousness is sometimes conceived as God himself, sometimes as God's gift. Thus a problem was foreshadowed which has persisted to the present.

Particularly in later Judaism, the Spirit is strongly personalized and is represented as speaking, warning, lamenting, rejoicing, consoling, and the like. Thus it is God who acts. Yet

[1] Eduard Schweizer and others, *Spirit of God,* trans. A. E. Harvey (London: Adam and Charles Black, 1960), p. 7. I have found this volume in Kittel's "Bible Key Words" series very helpful, and much of this section is based on it.

to the rabbinic writer, the gift of the Spirit is the reward of obedience. When bestowed, the Spirit inspires the just man still further to holiness of life. When the devout man sins, the Spirit departs from him.

In the past, the great figures in the history of Israel had possessed the Spirit to an exceptional degree. For the present, the rabbis in a vein suggestive of our contemporary pessimism tended to mourn the departure rather than rejoice in the presence of the Spirit. As for the future, the coming Messiah will possess the supreme gifts of the Spirit,

> the spirit of wisdom and understanding,
> the spirit of counsel and might,
> the spirit of knowledge and the fear of
> the Lord. (Isa. 11:2.)

In the Last Age the ransomed righteous will receive from God or his Messiah the Spirit of God, and with it moral renewal. In rabbinic thought the Spirit, though conceived in both personal and impersonal terms, is never identified with the Messiah or with an angelic heavenly being.[2]

In the apocryphal pre-Christian writings there is the same note of high expectancy that when the Messiah comes, he will be endowed with the Spirit of God to do his winnowing and redeeming work. Yet there is more confidence than in the rabbinical writings that even here and now the Spirit may be granted to men. There is also more attention given to the conception of the Spirit as the divine agent in creation, which in rabbinic literature is overshadowed by the conception of

[2] Schweizer, *ibid.*, pp. 12, 15.

the Spirit as the bearer of revelation and the endowment of the faithful.

From the Dead Sea scrolls it is apparent that in later Judaism there was a strong movement in the direction of conceiving the Spirit in both personal and ethical terms. Furthermore, there was a linkage of the Spirit with the Good in a metaphysical dualism acquired from Persian influence, a cosmic struggle in which the Spirit is present as the sustaining and enabling power of God against the powers of Evil. The *Manual of Discipline* says much of two spirits permeating and contending for man, a spirit of light and a spirit of darkness, of truth and of wickedness. The element of decision involved in every human life is here emphasized, but with stress also on man's living the good life, not by his own strength but by the power of God.

b. *The Spirit becomes the Holy Spirit.* The New Testament marks an all-important transition. We have noted that in the Old Testament "holy" is simply an adjective, used with Spirit only twice (or three times if one counts separately the repetitions found in Isa. 63:10, 11). In the New Testament the references to "the Spirit" or "the Spirit of God" continue in great profusion. Along with these there are also nearly one hundred references to the Holy Spirit. Henry P. Van Dusen has thus enumerated the frequency of use of these and other related terms:

The vocabulary of the New Testament is not uniform in referring to the Spirit. Of the more than three hundred (335) uses, over half (220) speak simply of "Spirit" or "the Spirit," while the term "Holy Spirit" which had occurred only twice in the Old Testament appears ninety-one times, "The Spirit of God" or "the Spirit of the Lord" or "the Spirit of the Father" nineteen times, and "the Spirit of Christ" five times.[3]

This frequency of reference marks the Holy Spirit as an essential New Testament idea, an element to be taken seriously even if it had not assumed central importance in the Christian doctrine of the Trinity.

Any consideration of this concept immediately brings to the foreground a problem perviously suggested. Shall we refer to the Holy Spirit as "He" or "It"? In other words, is the Spirit to be thought of as God himself, or as an attribute of the divine nature, or as the gift of God to those on whom he bestows it? We have noted that the translators of the Revised Standard Version have tried to designate the spirit (i.e., the nature) of God as an attribute of the divine being by using lower case type. Yet the context often fails to make the distinction clear. In New Testament interpretation the problem becomes the more important because of subsequent centuries of association of the Holy Spirit with the Trinity. To many, it would seem highly inappropriate to speak of the Holy Spirit except with the masculine personal pronoun that we use for God himself as a personal being.

The biblical writers, whether of the Old or New Testaments, did not solve this problem for us. The reason is that they were not metaphysicians interested in the drawing of such distinctions. What they were concerned about was the vital relation of the Spirit to human life and experience, and to this they witnessed with great ardor. They were fully convinced of the reality, the power, and the fruits of the

[3] Van Dusen, *Spirit, Son and Father*, p. 52.

Spirit; it apparently did not occur to them to ask for further definitions.

As a result, the Holy Spirit is referred to in various contexts in the New Testament, some of which seem to identify the Holy Spirit with God, others with Christ, and still others with the gift of God as supernatural power or insight, or with the life-giving work of Christ.

Accordingly, as we trace the development of references to the Holy Spirit through the New Testament, we shall use either the personal or the impersonal pronoun as the context seems to call for it. This is not to deny the validity of the Christian doctrine of the Trinity or to prejudge its meaning. On the contrary, if we are to understand with any clearness the place of the third member of the Trinity, we must note the steps by which it took on its meaning. This is the only way to deal faithfully with the term "Holy Spirit" as it was assuming meaning in living experience.

We cannot expect all the ambiguities to be removed. They are there to the end of the story. That the nature of the Holy Spirit had not been settled by the close of the New Testament period is evident from the statement of an outstanding authority. In Hastings' *Encyclopedia of Religion and Ethics*, R. Birch Hoyle gives a summary of historical research on the subject in which he says:

The apostolic age bequested to its successors four views of the Holy Spirit: (1) as an attribute of God without hypostatization; (2) as an impersonal energy or operation; (3) as a gift, expressed in impersonal terms; (4) as a Person with distinct hypostatization. The last was kept prominent before the Church by the baptismal formula (Mt. 28:19), the constant association of the

Holy Spirit with the Father and the Son as the object of faith and worship, and the expositions of the faith such as meet us in the various early forms of the so-called Apostles' Creed.[4]

If this was the legacy bequeathed by the apostolic age to its successors, by what stages within the New Testament did these developments take place? This must now be our inquiry.

2. THE SPIRIT IN THE FIRST THREE GOSPELS

Another problem immediately confronts us. Were we to follow the order in which the books of the New Testament were written, we should have to begin with Paul's letters. Here the Holy Spirit, though not yet an official doctrine, was present with vivifying and transforming power. Yet it was the life and ministry of Jesus, his death, resurrection, and his living presence that created the Church and gave rise to that vibrant faith which created the New Testament, including Paul's letters.

It seems wise, therefore, to begin with that part of the New Testament which gives our most authentic record of the words and ministry of Jesus. Where it seems called for, we shall note the influence of the early Church in the formation of the record that is found in the Synoptic Gospels.

The first thing noted as one looks in any good concordance is the scarcity of references to either the Spirit of God or the Holy Spirit[5] in the passages of the first three Gospels that

---

[4] "Spirit (Holy), Spirit of God," *Encyclopedia of Religion and Ethics* (New York: Charles Scribner's Sons, 1951), XI, 796.

[5] Or the Holy Ghost if the concordance is for the King James Version.

record the words of Jesus. There are more of these references in the passages *about* him, and the number increases greatly in the Gospel of John, Acts, and the letters of Paul. The references continue in the other epistles and in Revelation. Yet in Matthew, Mark, and Luke, aside from parallel references and the quotation from the sixty-first chapter of Isaiah with which Jesus began his ministry, the words recorded as spoken by Jesus contain but five references to the Holy Spirit and one to the Spirit of God.

Opinions differ as to which of these may be interpolations from the thought of the early Church. This is probably true of the baptismal formula in Matthew 28:19, since it represents a fairly advanced stage in the crystallizing of the Church's ritual. In two passages, the parallel form in another Gospel drops out the reference to the Spirit. Thus, Matthew's "If it is by the Spirit of God that I cast out demons" (Matt. 12:28) becomes in Luke, "If it is by the finger of God" (Luke 11:20). On the other hand, Luke's "How much more will the heavenly Father give the Holy Spirit to those who ask him?" (Luke 11:13) becomes in Matthew, "Give good things" (Matt. 7:11). The possibility is at least open that the alternate reading is the more authentic. Again, in reference to the inspiration of David in a quoted passage, Mark renders it "inspired by the Holy Spirit" (Mark 12:36) while Matthew says simply "inspired by the Spirit" (Matt. 22:43), which would be entirely in keeping with Old Testament usage.

Two other passages are of special importance because they are found in all three of the Synoptic Gospels. One of these is Jesus' counsel and word of encouragement to his followers in the face of opposition. In Mark the passage reads, "And when they bring you to trial and deliver you up, do not be anxious beforehand what you are to say; but say whatever is given you in that hour, for it is not you who speak, but the Holy Spirit" (Mark 13:11). Matthew renders it, "For it is not you who speak, but the Spirit of your Father speaking through you" (Matt. 10:20). Luke's version is, "For the Holy Spirit will teach you in that very hour what you ought to say" (Luke 12:12). The opinions of scholars on these variant readings range from dismissal of all three as interpolations of the early Church to acceptance of them as authentic foreshadowings of the coming Paraclete as this is found in the Fourth Gospel and especially in John 15:26.

This brings us to the final passage, the teaching about blasphemy against the Holy Spirit. While often regarded as the most difficult to interpret, it is generally considered the most clearly authentic. Even here there are variations in the form. While all three passages (Mark 3:28-30; Matt. 12:31, 32; Luke 12:10) contain references to the Holy Spirit, Matthew refers also, as the Old Testament might, to "the Spirit," and apparently uses the terms interchangeably. In Matthew and Luke a contrast is drawn between blasphemy against the Son of man and against the Holy Spirit, which seems to indicate that Jesus was not identifying himself with the Holy Spirit.[6] What he appears to be affirming in this "hard saying" is the utter seriousness of sinning against the light of God's

---

[6] George S. Hendry in *The Holy Spirit in Christian Theology* (Philadelphia: Westminster Press, 1956), p. 26, declares, "There is no reference in the New Testament to any work of the Spirit apart from Christ. The Spirit is, in an exclusive sense, the Spirit of Christ." While I should agree that the Spirit is not mentioned in the New Testament except as it is in some way related to Christ, this passage seems to negate his second sentence.

51

Spirit, "the sin described by Isaiah as calling good evil and evil good, putting darkness for light and light for darkness, bitter for sweet and sweet for bitter (Isaiah 5:20)." [7] Where there is no repentance through hardness of heart and human presumption, there can be no forgiveness.

What is to be concluded from this examination? The first and most obvious comment is that we do not have all the words of Jesus, and among those reported as spoken by him, we cannot be sure of exactly what he said. Nevertheless, it seems probable, both that he *did* speak of the Holy Spirit in reference to matters of great seriousness, and that he spoke thus sparingly. It is also entirely possible that in his own references to the Spirit, "holy" was simply a descriptive adjective as in Psalms 51:11 and Isaiah 63:10, 11.

That Jesus should have spoken of the Spirit, even though the early Church may from its own usage have prefixed "Holy," is perfectly understandable. The mind of Jesus was saturated with the Old Testament Scriptures; his heart was attuned to the Spirit of God as no prophet's before him had ever been. What is strange about the record is that he did not speak more often. Even granting that some references may have been lost, the number recorded is surprisingly few.

In the words of the Synoptic writers about Jesus, more references to the Holy Spirit are found. But even here, they are not numerous, and they appear almost entirely at the beginning of the record in regard to his birth, baptism, temptation, and the commencement of his ministry. According to

[7] Lindsay Dewar, *The Holy Spirit and Modern Thought* (New York: Harper & Bros., 1960), p. 19. He also makes a case on the basis of this passage for the recognition by Jesus of the light of the Holy Spirit in every man through conscience. I doubt that Jesus was being analytical to this extent.

Luke, the birth of Jesus was preceded by the coming of the Holy Spirit to Elizabeth, Zechariah, and Simeon (Luke 1:41, 67; 2:25). According to both Matthew and Luke, the Holy Spirit is promised to Mary as the source of the birth of her child (Matt. 1:18; Luke 1:35). All three of these Gospels, and John as well, speak of the descent of the Spirit of God like a dove at Jesus' baptism (Matt. 3:16; Mark 1:10; Luke 3:22; John 1:32). He is led up by the Spirit into the wilderness to be tempted by the devil (Matt. 4:1; Mark 1:12; Luke 4:1) and returns at the end of this time "in the power of the Spirit" (Luke 4:14) to begin his ministry. Once afterward we find Luke saying that "he rejoiced in the Holy Spirit" at the exultant return of the seventy, and was prompted thereby to offer a prayer of thanksgiving to the Father (Luke 10:21).

These are significant passages, which indicate that the concept of the Holy Spirit had penetrated the thought of the Synoptists. Furthermore, this localization around the birth of Jesus and the beginning of his ministry indicates that they believed these events to be in a very special sense the work of the Spirit, God present and God acting. Yet the scarcity of such references in regard to the later events justifies the characterization, "the silence of the Synoptists." [8]

Several explanations are possible, each supplementary to the others rather than exclusive. One is that Jesus felt his own relation to the Father to be one of such immediacy that he felt no need to speak of the Spirit as a mediating agent.

---

[8] The title of a chapter in J. E. Fison's *The Blessing of the Holy Spirit* (New York: Longmans, Green & Co., 1950), pp. 81-109. Van Dusen, *Spirit, Son and Father,* 53, 56 stresses the frequency of references to the Holy Spirit by the Synoptists in connection with the major events of Jesus' life. Fison's judgment seems to me the more realistic.

To him the Spirit *was* the Father, and while the terms could be used interchangeably, it was the Father's all-encompassing, gracious love that occupied the foreground of his thought.

Closely akin to this is Jesus' central message of the kingdom, in which in parable after parable is stressed the need of trust in God and of moral obedience to the Father as man's highest goal. This, to be sure, does not exclude the quest for the Spirit as God's "good gift" (Matt. 7:11). Yet it is a quest to be guided and directed by the mandates of the kingdom.

By the time the Synoptists wrote, there was already in the Church a good deal of speaking with tongues and other forms of emotional effervescence in connection with what was thought to be the power of the Spirit. As we shall see presently, this bore more than a little resemblance to the ecstatic utterances of the "prophesying" in the early Old Testament. It is significant that Jesus never indulged in such excesses, according to the Gospels' reports of either his words or deeds. This indicates both his own deeper rootage in uninterrupted fellowship with God and possibly also his reluctance to speak much of the Spirit because of current misunderstandings of how the Spirit worked.

Still another possible explanation relates to the complex problem of Jesus' own messianic consciousness. After his death and resurrection, it was natural enough for his disciples to think of the Holy Spirit both as the successor to the Jesus they had known and as the presence of the living Christ. For him to have attempted this during his lifetime would either, on the one hand, have been a premature letting out of his messianic secret or on the other, sheer presumption if he did not regard himself as the promised Messiah. In either case, there is sufficient ground for his not making this identification.

Regardless of the fact that Jesus did not speak much of the Holy Spirit or claim for himself the Spirit's presence, it is undeniable that he was Spirit-filled and Spirit-led. Those who wrote about him, both in the Gospels and elsewhere in the New Testament, witness to this fact both directly and by continuous implication. It is crucial to our understanding of both Son and Spirit.

As for the Synoptists' own silence as they recorded the events of Jesus' ministry, it was natural that they should have been so impressed with the marvel of his coming and the reality of his Sonship that references to the Holy Spirit should crowd the earlier pages. It is not so easy to see why, in view of the miracles Jesus performed and his frequent exorcism of evil spirits, we should find only the one reference, "If it is by the Spirit of God [the finger of God] that I cast out demons, then the kingdom of God has come upon you" (Matt. 12:28; Luke 11:20).

Yet this passage may itself be something of a clue to the silence of the Synoptists. As the ministry of Jesus progressed, his deeds were those of compassion and helpfulness rather than spectacular achievement. His words were mainly about the kingdom, and the justice and love of the Father, and man's duty in faith and obedience to the love commandment, rather than about the Spirit. If this is a fair deduction from the scarcity of the quotations cited by the Synoptists, it was natural that in speaking about him they should have made few references to the Holy Spirit except in the initial validation of his ministry.

Thus, we find that in the first three Gospels, awareness of

the Holy Spirit is present, but present primarily in the background. For its presence in the foreground we must look to other parts of the New Testament.

3. PENTECOST

We shall defer looking at the Fourth Gospel until later, not only because it was probably written considerably later, but because Luke-Acts originally was one book. Thus, the story of the giving of the Holy Spirit at Pentecost stands in direct continuation of Luke's account.

The continuity is often traced by regarding Jesus' promise of the Holy Spirit in John 14:25, 26 and 15:26 as being fulfilled in the second chapter of Acts. It is not necessary to deny such a connection, for the marvelous words of comfort and hope spoken in the Last Supper discourse doubtless have some historical foundation. Yet the more immediate antecedent from the standpoint of Luke-Acts is found in Luke 24:49, "And behold, I send the promise of my Father upon you; but stay in the city, until you are clothed with power from on high." This ties directly into Acts 1:4, 5 which refers again to the promise of the Father but adds the note, "John baptized with water, but before many days you shall be baptized with the Holy Spirit." The repetition of the promise in Acts 1:8, "You shall receive power when the Holy Spirit has come upon you," is followed immediately by the commission to witness to all the world.

The second chapter of Acts tells how this promise was fulfilled with striking and transforming significance. The remainder of the New Testament, and the existence of the Church to the present, indicate the results. While there are some disputable elements in the story, the main picture is remarkably clear.

First, the disciples were together and waiting. The company apparently included the twelve, Matthias having been chosen by lot to replace Judas, though he is never heard from again, and enough others to make about one hundred and twenty. Probably all of these were Jews, and it is not surprising that they should have assembled to observe together the Jewish festival of Pentecost, fifty days after the Passover. Yet in the hearts of those who had known and loved Jesus there was also a great expectancy born of their resurrection faith.

Just what happened we do not know. The biblical symbolism of "the rushing of a mighty wind" and "tongues as of fire, distributed and resting on each one of them," verses 2, 3, has its analogies in the Old Testament, where the divine *ruach* was originally wind, and Moses had received his commission at the burning bush (Exod. 3:2). Here, however, is the suggestion of something overpowering and marvelous that made their faces radiant with a new joy, and that seemed to illumine the total scene. Whatever it was that happened, it seems certain that, as Paul puts it in another setting, they were "aglow with the Spirit" (Rom. 12:11).

The marvel continues with the account of their speaking in various national languages. Was this the glossolalia, or speaking in tongues, which by the time Luke wrote was already a common phenomenon in the early Church? It is usually so interpreted, but the problem is complicated by the fact that nowhere else is any mention made of the ability to communicate in foreign languages. Whatever the answer, a deeper meaning is found in the power of the Spirit to unite the most disparate groups about a common center. Granting that all were Jews, "devout men from every nation under heaven," and that most of them understood the *koine* Greek and Aramaic which were the common languages of the day, it was not linguistics but a great new sense of the Spirit's presence that united them. Glossolalia was regarded by Paul as among the Spirit's lesser gifts, distinctly subordinate both to love and to speaking with understanding (I Cor. 12–14). What seems to be central in the story of Pentecost is the power of the Holy Spirit to break down "the dividing walls of hostility" (Eph. 2:14) among those present. It becomes very meaningful in our time to anyone who has ever sat in a great ecumenical service of worship and, without understanding the languages being used, has felt the pervasive power of the one Holy Spirit to transcend all barriers.

Next we find Peter, a leader by nature but up to this time not eloquent, preaching a remarkable sermon. He appeals to the wisdom of the past, quoting Joel's prophecy; he finds its promise fulfilled in the "mighty works," crucifixion, and resurrection of Jesus of Nazareth. It comes to a great climax in the words, "Let all the house of Israel therefore know assuredly that God has made him both Lord and Christ, this Jesus whom you crucified."

Further results appear in the call to repentance, the response of the people, and their baptism up to the number of three thousand souls. That the fruits were genuine is evidenced by the continuance of fellowship in teaching and learning, in eating together, and in common worship. The fact that they "had all things in common" is not to be taken as a sanctification of anything known today as communism, but as indication of the stirrings of the Spirit to a great mutual concern in things material as well as of the spirit. There is a triumphant and invigorating note in the concluding words of the chapter:

And day by day, attending the temple together and breaking bread in their homes, they partook of food with glad and generous hearts, praising God and having favor with all the people. And the Lord added to their number day by day those who were being saved. (Acts 2:46, 47.)

Could the churches say this today, how much less the need of talk of a "post-Christian era"!

Because of the great events of Pentecost, and still more because of what resulted from it, it is customary to speak of Pentecost as "the birthday of the Church." With this judgment I concur, provided we do not overlook the fact that there could have been no Pentecost without the presence of the Spirit of God in the life and ministry, death and resurrection of Jesus. And back of this, the divine Spirit was present to direct the destinies of the chosen people of Israel, brooding over them even as he brooded over chaos to create the cosmos. There are new beginnings, of which the creation of the Church of Christ by the Holy Spirit was a great new event. Yet in God's providence there are no absolute beginnings, for his Spirit is eternal and eternally at work.

Again, the corporate nature of the Spirit's coming at Pentecost, resulting in the corporate fellowship of the Church as the Spirit's primary medium, is often emphasized. And again I am willing to accede to this, provided it is not overdone. Those who are most concerned to stress this note are prone to depreciate the presence of the Holy Spirit not only in mystical experience but in individual conversion. There are

59

pitfalls in all of these approaches. Yet as we look at Pentecost, what stands out with clarity is that the Holy Spirit came to individuals-in-community. Eliminate either the experience, past, present, and future, of the persons involved or their corporate unity through the action of the Holy Spirit, and there would be no Pentecost.

To sum up, the Spirit came with *power*. The "power of the resurrection" that had been promised was with Christ's followers in a new and vibrant sense, and they became a witnessing community, courageous and undaunted by obstacles.

The Spirit came with *a moral urgency* that linked holiness with service and Jesus' teaching of the love commandments with spiritual gifts.

The Spirit came *in continuity with the historical past*. It is no accident that Jews were together observing a Jewish religious festival, or that Peter quoted an Old Testament prophet as his base in Scripture.

The Spirit came in *more immediate continuity with Jesus*. The Holy Spirit meant thereafter the Spirit of God, as it had previously, but also the Spirit of Jesus Christ.

The Spirit came to *individuals within a fellowship*. It came initially to 120 persons to knit them together in a life-transforming unity; it came to more and more persons as others were touched by the Spirit's power. Thus, it was neither the possession of these individuals separately nor of the group corporately, but of *both*.

And, finally, "the fellowship of the Holy Spirit" *gave rise to the fellowship of the Christian Church*. It did not immediately give rise to the institutional forms of the Church. It did not guarantee that the successors of Peter were later to be known as Popes, or even that "the breaking of bread and the prayers" were to become the Eucharistic sacrifice and the liturgy, though there is a connection in the elaboration of these acts. What it did establish, with a vitality that has fluctuated but never died out, is the fellowship of Christ's followers which even today by the power of the Holy Spirit could become a world-transforming community.

What happened to these Jewish followers of Jesus on that historic day and immediately thereafter was soon to break through the barriers of race and religion to become a faith for the Gentiles also. How this came about through the work of the Holy Spirit, and how the Holy Spirit came to be identified in the early Church with the living Christ, must be our next inquiry.

IV

THE HOLY SPIRIT
IN
THE EARLY CHURCH

It is in the remainder of the book of Acts, Paul's letters, and the Gospel of John that we see most clearly both the results of Pentecost and the nuances of thought that came over the Church's understanding of the Holy Spirit. It is in this order that we shall examine the record.

1. THE RECORD IN THE BOOK OF ACTS

In striking contrast to the relative silence in the first three Gospels, the remainder of Acts after Pentecost abounds in references to the Holy Spirit. In view of the fact that it was written by the author of the third Gospel, only Pentecost itself can explain the difference. The references appear in almost every chapter.

What, then, did the Holy Spirit's presence mean to those first Christians?

As in Pentecost, it meant *an influx of power.* At some points this is represented as the power to work miracles, as in Peter's healing of the lame man at the Beautiful Gate of the temple by saying to him, "In the name of Jesus Christ of Nazareth, walk" (Acts 3:6). So evident was this strange power that Simon the magician of Samaria, half believing and half self-seeking, tried to buy it (Acts 8:9-24).

However, it is in the greater miracle of courage and an amazing *fidelity in witness under opposition* that the power of the Holy Spirit is most often and most clearly seen. Peter's defense when arrested for healing the lame man (Acts 4:8-12); his "We must obey God rather than men" when imprisoned and told to keep silent (Acts 5:27-32); Stephen's sermon which enraged the traditionalists because of his plain speaking and his death "full of the Holy Spirit" (Acts 7) are dramatic examples.

In the narrative that fills the book of Acts, we begin also to find a gift of the Holy Spirit which is central to its subsequent meaning; namely, *guidance and illumination*. After Peter's vision, or dream, of a great sheet let down from heaven in which were "unclean" animals he was bidden to kill and eat, followed immediately by the arrival of messengers from the Gentile Cornelius, he knew that Jewish exclusiveness must give way before the gospel. This turning point in the history of Christianity Peter records in the simple words, "And the Spirit told me to go with them without hesitation" (Acts 11:12). The problem was not yet fully solved, and in the crucial Jerusalem conference over the circumcision of the Gentile Christians we find the same note sounded in the apostolic letter that was sent to Antioch, "It has seemed good to the Holy Spirit and to us. . ." (Acts 15:28).

In the subsequent events connected with the extension of the gospel to the Gentiles, there are frequent references to the Holy Spirit which link together personal conversion with accessions to the fellowship that were marked by *baptism with water.* As Peter was speaking in the house of Cornelius and "the Holy Spirit fell on all who heard the word" (Acts 10:44), the Jewish believers were amazed, for "they heard them speaking in tongues and extolling God" (vs. 46). Peter then declared, "Can any one forbid water for baptizing these people who have received the Holy Spirit just as we have?" The result was baptism in the name of Jesus Christ (vss. 46-48). Peter speaks in the same vein at the Jerusalem council, but there is no reference here either to baptism or to speaking with tongues: "And God who knows the heart bore witness to them, giving them the Holy Spirit just as he did to us; and he made no distinction between us and them, but cleansed their hearts by faith" (Acts 15:8-9).

Numerous references to baptism in the book of Acts indicate that it was a common practice in the early Church. So, too, was *the laying on of hands,* from which were later to come the rites of both confirmation and ministerial ordination. Yet there is no evidence that either of these practices, and even less the speaking with tongues, was the invariable accompaniment of receiving the Holy Spirit. It was when God had "cleansed their hearts by faith" that the Holy Spirit came. Then baptism followed as the seal of the Spirit's, and the Church's, admission to the fellowship of Christian believers. This is dramatically shown in the story of the conversion of the Ethiopian eunuch as Philip at the Spirit's behest interpreted to him the Scriptures and "told him the good news of Jesus" (Acts 8:26-39).

Sometimes, but not always, the laying on of hands seems to have been a supplement to baptism. This we find in the case of the Samaritans to whom Peter and John were sent (Acts 8:14-17). It appears also in the story of Paul's encoun-

ter with those at Ephesus who had "never even heard that
there is a Holy Spirit," having received only John's baptism,
and Paul's correction of this circumstance by baptizing them
in the name of the Lord Jesus (Acts 19:1-7). We are told,
"And when Paul had laid his hands upon them, the Holy
Spirit came on them; and they spoke with tongues and
prophesied" (vs. 6). It has been argued from these incidents that in the early Church confirmation was a primary
medium of receiving the Holy Spirit.[1] This assumption seems
to me unwarranted, for on the same basis the speaking with
tongues would need to be viewed as normal procedure and
endowed with sacerdotal efficacy.

A vital aspect of the work of the Holy Spirit, foreshadowed
in the commission that came with the promise of power in
Acts 1:8, was the guidance that came as *a call to missionary
service.* An early manifestation of this which was to bear
much fruit—indeed, an apparently minor incident which in
God's providence was to have major consequences—is seen in
the decision of the Jerusalem church to send to Antioch Barnabas, "a good man, full of the Holy Spirit and of faith"
(Acts 11:24). Then came Barnabas' trip to Tarsus to look
for Saul and his bringing him to Antioch; the coming of
famine; and the decision to send relief to Jerusalem by the
hands of Barnabas and Saul (vss. 25-30). Two chapters later
comes the launching of Paul's world-shaping missionary jour-
neys by the Spirit-led action of the church at Antioch:

While they were worshiping the Lord and fasting, the Holy
Spirit said, "Set apart for me Barnabas and Saul for the work

[1] Dewar, *The Holy Spirit and Modern Thought,* pp. 51-57.

to which I have called them." Then after fasting and praying they laid their hands on them and sent them off.

So, being sent out by the Holy Spirit, they went down to Seleucia; and from there they sailed to Cyprus. (Acts 13:2-4.)

This guidance was to continue throughout Paul's many travels. Sometimes the guidance from the Holy Spirit was to refrain from proposed action rather than to act. The following passage is significant both because it leads up to Paul's Macedonian call and because it gives an instance, rare in Acts but more common in Paul's letters, of the identification of the Holy Spirit with the Spirit of Jesus: "And they went through the region of Phrygia and Galatia, having been forbidden by the Holy Spirit to speak the word in Asia. And when they had come opposite Mysia, they attempted to go into Bithynia, but the Spirit of Jesus did not allow them; so, passing by Mysia, they went down to Troas" (Acts 16:6-8).

The passages quoted illustrate the fact that as yet there was no systematized doctrine of the Holy Spirit, or any clear indication of which pronoun to use. We are told repeatedly of persons who were "full of the Holy Spirit" (Acts 6:3, 5; 7:55; 11:24; 13:9, 52); of others who "received" the Holy Spirit or of those on whom the Holy Spirit "fell" or "was poured out" (Acts 5:32; 8:15-18; 9:17; 10:44-47; 11:15-17; 15:8; 19:2, 6). In such passages, it would be awkward to substitute the term "God," for the context clearly suggests a marvelous new influx of grace—a more-than-human power and illumination which was the gift of God to those who became Christian believers. Its effect, though occasionally associated with a charismatic speaking with tongues, is most clearly shown in the power to witness to their faith and to live together in a joyous and supporting fellowship. "So the church throughout all Judea and Galilee and Samaria had peace and was built up; and walking in the fear of the Lord and in the comfort of the Holy Spirit it was multiplied" (Acts 9:31).

While as yet there was no clear-cut identification of the Holy Spirit as a personal entity, there are passages which look in this direction. The Holy Spirit is personalized and referred to either as speaking or as being spoken to in Ananias' lying defiance (Acts 5:3), Peter's directive to visit Cornelius (Acts 11:12), the call of Barnabas and Saul (Acts 13:2); and in instructions and warnings given to Paul (Acts 16:6; 20:23, 28; 21:11). The degree to which the Old Testament idea of the Spirit of God had now become identified with the Holy Spirit is suggested in Paul's concluding statement in the book of Acts, where he introduces a quotation from the sixth chapter of Isaiah with the words, "The Holy Spirit was right in saying to your fathers through Isaiah the prophet . . ." (Acts 28:25).

2. THE LETTERS OF PAUL

References to the Holy Spirit appear in Paul's writing in great profusion. He refers to the Spirit in one way or another more than a hundred times. While what he says still falls short of a systematic doctrine of the Trinity and of the Holy Spirit's place within it, he gives intimations which are very important both for theology and for Christian living.

Paul's letters, the earliest contemporary writing in the New

Testament, were written midway between the events of the crucifixion and resurrection of Jesus, followed by Pentecost, and the writing of the Gospels. It is an amazing evidence of the work of the Holy Spirit that the little Christian fellowship not only survived but continued to grow during the ten or fifteen years before Paul began his ministry. His writing presupposes this background, though he did much to shape the foreground of the Church.

We must now note certain definite points of change, not wholly new but shifts in emphasis, from what Luke records in the book of Acts.

To begin where we left off in the preceding section, Paul's references to the Holy Spirit are almost wholly in *personal terms*. No longer is the Spirit "poured out" or are persons "filled with" the Spirit; rather, the Spirit dwells in us, leads, bears witness, helps us in our weakness, intercedes for us, has a mind (Rom. 8:11, 14, 16, 26, 27). Unlike the greater part of the references in the Synoptic Gospels and in Acts, the term God can be substituted, and it becomes quite natural to speak of the Spirit as "He."

To this significant fact is added another of great importance. Not only can the Holy Spirit and God be used as *interchangeable terms,* but so can "Christ" or "the Lord" or "the Spirit of Jesus Christ." This identification becomes complete in, "Now the Lord is the Spirit, and where the Spirit of the Lord is, there is freedom" (II Cor. 3:17). The context makes it clear that it is Christ who is being referred to as the Lord, since a contrast is drawn between God's self-disclosure in Moses and in Christ. It is the risen Christ to whom Paul refers, but it is the risen Christ in direct continuity with the

Jesus whom men had known upon earth. In the next verse the identification is repeated with the further affirmation that through the Lord who is the Spirit "we all, with unveiled face, beholding the glory of the Lord, are being changed into his likeness from one degree of glory to another" (II Cor. 3:18).

This is but a short step away from another note of great significance in Paul's understanding of the Spirit; namely, the *ethical qualities* which the Spirit asks of and imparts to the Christian. This is epitomized in one of the greatest verses of the Bible, ranking close to the Beatitudes as a summary of the Christian graces, "But the fruit of the Spirit is love, joy, peace, patience, kindness, goodness, faithfulness, gentleness, self-control; against such there is no law" (Gal. 5:22).

The same thought is suggested in Paul's references to "the mind of Christ." This certainly does not mean the intellectual qualities of Jesus, but the total revelation of God in the moral and spiritual person of the Jesus who was now conceived as the Christ. As such, the mind of Christ is both the Christian's assurance and the demand that is placed upon him.

As Paul uses the term, *the mind of Christ* apparently means the disclosure of God in the incarnate Lord. It also means the Spirit of God that is the Spirit of Jesus Christ. The term appears twice in his letters, both times in close conjunction with references to the Spirit. In, "But we have the mind of Christ" (I Cor. 2:16) the statement stands at the end of an eloquent passage on the Spirit of God as this teaches the spirit of man. In, "Have this mind among yourselves, which you have in Christ Jesus" (Phil. 2:5) this is significantly placed between counsels to human love, sympathy, and service and Paul's portrayal of Christ's willingness to humble

69

himself in order to become incarnate in human form. Here the reference to the Spirit is more indirect, but the identification with Christ is implied in the opening words of the passages, "So if there is any encouragement in Christ, any incentive of love, any participation in the Spirit, any affection and sympathy, complete my joy by being of the same mind, having the same love, being in full accord and of one mind" (Phil. 2:1).

However, it is in the discussion of spiritual gifts in First Corinthians, chapters twelve through fourteen, that Paul reaches his greatest insights. This is true even though in the ode to love in the thirteenth chapter, neither Christ nor the Holy Spirit is expressly mentioned. The connection is closer than is commonly realized when its beauty and universal truth lead to its being quoted out of context.

The preceding chapter speaks of various gifts "inspired by one and the same Spirit, who apportions to each one individually as he wills" (I Cor. 12:11). Such a variety of gifts leads to various interconnected functions in the Church, the body of Christ. The same note is taken up more specifically in the fourteenth chapter, where speaking with tongues is not disparaged but is definitely subordinated to prophesying and to speaking intelligibly for the sake of instructing others. Paul's practical wisdom appears in the injunction, "Since you are eager for manifestations of the Spirit, strive to excel in building up the church" (I Cor. 14:12).

Yet it is in the love chapter itself that *the identification of the Holy Spirit with Christ* is most fully made, though it is not so stated. We said earlier that Jesus, though he spoke little of the Spirit, was certainly Spirit-filled and Spirit-led. The love chapter is a perfect description of "the mind of Christ." [2] Where else did Paul get this insight? For Saul the rigorous Pharisee to have written it would have been an impossibility; it flows naturally from the pen of Paul the transformed Christian.

This is not to say that Paul was trying consciously to epitomize the life or the teaching of Jesus. More than likely he was not. Yet so deeply had the Spirit implanted this message upon his heart that it flowed forth in beauty and power. Implied throughout in this "more excellent way" is the goal of love which every follower of Christ ought to set before him and desire earnestly as the supreme gift of God to the human spirit.

We find, then, that not only does Paul identify the work of the Holy Spirit with the work of Christ, but this identification is made in the most highly ethical terms. The Spirit of God had been "ethicized" before in the Old Testament, in the rabbinical writings, and in the pre-Pauline church as seen in the early chapters of Acts. What Paul does is to lift up the demands and the gifts of love as the message of Christ through the Holy Spirit. Paul does not raise, or attempt to answer, the theoretical question of the relation of the Holy Spirit to the Godhead, but he does in experience speak interchangeably of God, Christ, and the Holy Spirit.

This is not Paul's only contribution, though the others to be mentioned are derivative from this major one. A further note of great importance is his taking the activity of the Holy

---

[2] While its being spoken by Jesus in the movie *The Greatest Story Ever Told* distorts the account in the Gospels, the producer had some justification.

71

Spirit out of the realm of the occasional and the dramatic and placing it *within the everyday life of the Christian.*

Previously the work of the Spirit had been recognized in unusual events, such as speaking with tongues or the ecstatic glow of Pentecost. We have seen that the early Church also found the Spirit giving guidance at points of crucial decision. Paul does not disparage any of this, and he speaks of himself in his conversion experience as having been "caught up to the third heaven" and as having had visions and revelations (II Cor. 12:1-4). Nevertheless, it is in the daily business of living that "to each is given the manifestation of the Spirit for the common good" (I Cor. 12:7). This may mean being apostles, prophets, teachers, workers of miracles, healers, helpers, administrators, speakers in tongues or their interpreters, for all have a place and the one Spirit bestows these gifts (I Cor. 12:4-11, 28-30).

These are gifts bestowed by the Spirit within the Church. Yet it is important to note that they are not given *by* the Church, or within the Church as an institution. It was within the fellowship of the Church that the Spirit spoke, and spoke to transform life in its totality.

This *radical transformation of life* is another of Paul's great contributions. And again we find the work of Christ identified with the work of the Holy Spirit. In the eighth chapter of Romans after Paul's vivid description, perhaps autobiographical, of the futile wrestle with sin that appears in the seventh, he comes through to a triumphant affirmation in the words, "There is therefore now no condemnation for those who are in Christ Jesus. For the law of the Spirit of life in Christ Jesus has set me free from the law of sin and death" (Rom.

8:1-2). This is identical in its import with, "Therefore, if any one is in Christ, he is a new creation; the old has passed away, behold, the new has come" (II Cor. 5:17). Both passages witness equally to the transformation of life which the committed Christian experiences in Christ, though in the first the Spirit is mentioned and not in the second. In either case, there is no piecemeal change indicated; it is life as a whole that is made over.

What does Paul mean by the phrase which he uses repeatedly, to be "in Christ"? There are competent scholars who hold that this term, like "the fellowship of the Holy Spirit" in the apostolic benediction of Second Corinthians 13:14, means to be in the Church, that is, in the fellowship of the Christian community. I am unable to discern that this is what Paul means by either phrase, though he certainly expected and desired that Christian believers should affiliate with other Christians in work and witness and "maintain the unity of the Spirit in the bond of peace" (Eph. 4:3). Nor does the phrase "Christ mysticism" seem to me a very accurate description of what is meant by being "in Christ." Mysticism is of many sorts, and while communion with God, or Christ, or the Holy Spirit is an intelligible term, union of our human frailty in metaphysical oneness with the divine is neither intelligible nor Christian.

A simpler explanation is the more credible, and more relevant to our own present-day experience. When God through Christ (we may equally well say through the Holy Spirit) transforms a life and one becomes thereby a committed Christian, endeavoring thereafter to live the life of faith and love, he is a new man in Christ. Such a life must be nourished by public worship, by private communion with God in prayer, by works of love, and by a steady, undergirding sense of the divine presence throughout the whole of life. In this process of coming to Christ and living in Christ, the Church is a major factor, but it is not the sole agency.

As I read Paul, his primary concern was with evangelism, not in a narrow but in its broadest sense. He was a great theologian and administrator, but his "heart's desire and prayer to God" (Rom. 10:1) for all men was that they might be saved, that is, brought to acceptance of the gospel with the resulting transformation of life. He established churches and wrought mightily for "building up the body of Christ" (Eph. 4:12), even as he counseled other Christians to do. Yet he appears above all to have been concerned that those won to Christ should continue in the Christian way, empowered by "the grace of the Lord Jesus Christ and the love of God and the fellowship of the Holy Spirit."

If this be true, the judgment of H. Wheeler Robinson is well worth pondering:

The increasing recognition that the doctrine of the Holy Spirit is central in the Christian thought of the Apostle Paul (rather than the Rabbinical doctrine of "justification") marks a great advance in the interpretation of his Gospel. Every other conception of his is baptized into this, and most of all the concrete fact of history—the Cross of Christ. The whole life of the Christian, normal and abnormal, is brought within the sphere of the Holy Spirit.[3]

[3] *The Christian Experience of the Holy Spirit*, pp. 14 f.

3. THE GOSPEL OF JOHN

It is in the Fourth Gospel that the developments we have been tracing come to fruition. Opinions differ greatly as to the date and degree of authenticity of this Gospel. While it is usually thought to have been written around the end of the first century, some recent scholarship dates it as early as A.D. 70 and regards it, not as a supplement to the Synoptics, but as an independent witness.

The first three Gospels are generally regarded as the more historically dependable. There are marked differences in John. Not only are different incidents recorded, and different sequences among those common to the other Gospels, but that Jesus is the Christ, the Son of God, is assumed throughout without question and with no suggestion of messianic secrecy. Nevertheless, these differences do not exclude the possibility that some of the incidents and conversations, and particularly the words at the Last Supper, are based on authentic records. These are so full of love and deep understanding and so true to the spirit of Jesus that on any other basis their writing is a mystery. In any case, they speak words of guidance, comfort, and strength which not only the author of the Gospel, but we ourselves, feel it appropriate that Jesus should have spoken.

With reference to the presence of the Holy Spirit there is not full consistency, for the early part of the Gospel speaks of the Spirit as already present while the Last Supper discourse promises the Spirit's coming to take the place of Jesus after his approaching death. It is the latter that is the more distinctive, but let us note what can be gleaned from the earlier passages.

As in the Synoptics, the Spirit descends upon Jesus at his baptism. The declaration is made by John the Baptist that this is the Son of God, and that he will baptize, not with water like the Baptist himself, but with the Holy Spirit (John 1:29-34).

The next mention of the Spirit is in the interview with Nicodemus in the third chapter. The incident is very significant, for in the words ascribed to Jesus he links being "born of the Spirit" with entrance into the kingdom of God. The allusion to the wind which blows where it wills without our understanding may be intended as a reference to the Old Testament *ruach*. If it is, it is placed in the New Testament context of spiritual rebirth. The call to be "born anew" modulates into a discourse on the love of God who has sent his Son to make this possible. In this setting we find John 3:16, the most familiar and beloved words of the entire Bible, repeated today in many hundreds of languages around the world. Thus in a single context, though without either merger or sharply defined differentiation, we find the love of God, the sending of his Son, and the life-giving work of the Spirit. Furthermore, this implicit but undefined Trinity is here connected for the first time in the Fourth Gospel with a note which characterizes the message of this Gospel, the promise of eternal life to the Christian believer.

The next passage where the Spirit appears is in the conversation of Jesus with the woman at the well. Here the reference is verbally more indirect, for it appears only in, "God is spirit, and those who worship him must worship in spirit and truth" (John 4:24). The statement that "God is spirit" possibly reflects a Greek distinction between spirit and matter which by this time had become merged with Christian thought. Yet the assurance to this ignorant and unsavory character is virtually the same as to the educated Nicodemus, though now the analogy shifts from wind to water. The life-giving water that will quench the deepest thirsts of the spirit of man to "become in him a spring of water welling up to eternal life" (John 4:14) is from God the Father through the Son, and God is spirit.

Thereafter we find more references to the Son, but not again to the Spirit until the seventh chapter. There, almost as if the author of the Gospel had realized that there was some inconsistency between the Spirit as present and the Spirit as yet to come, we find him representing Jesus as saying publicly, "If any one thirst, let him come to me and drink. He who believes in me, as the scripture has said, 'Out of his heart shall flow rivers of living water.'" Then follow the words, as an author's comment, "Now this he said about the Spirit, which those who believed in him were to receive; for as yet the Spirit had not been given, because Jesus was not yet glorified" (John 7:37-39).

There is no further reference to the Spirit until the Last Supper discourse. There we find again and again the coming Paraclete, formerly translated "Comforter" but now rendered "Counselor" in the Revised Standard Version (John 14:15-18, 26; 15:26; 16:7-15). It is difficult to find an adequate term to express all that the Paraclete means as the helper of man in his deepest needs. In I John 2:1, where the same Greek word is used to describe "Jesus Christ the righteous," it is translated "advocate," and "advocate" is the term used in the New English Bible for the Fourth Gospel passages. But since our Lord spoke Aramaic rather than Greek, and we do not have his original words, the best way to grasp its meaning is to see what it is promised that the coming Paraclete will do.

The Counselor, we are told repeatedly, is the Spirit of truth. "But the Counselor, the Holy Spirit, whom the Father will send in my name, he will teach you all things, and bring to your remembrance all that I have said to you" (John 14: 26). "But when the Counselor comes, whom I shall send to you from the Father, even the Spirit of truth, who proceeds from the Father, he will bear witness to me" (John 15:26). "When the Spirit of truth comes, he will guide you into all the truth" (John 16:13). These passages are of great importance, for they promise not only the perpetuation of the memory of Jesus, without which there could be no Christian Church, but the continuing disclosures of truth which would supplement the revelation already given.

What is this promised "Spirit of truth"? Though neither Jesus nor the Evangelist defines it for us, we are not left in doubt as to its meaning. It is the life-giving certainty of the disclosure of the Father in the Son—the same sort of certainty that is intimated in, "I am the way, and the truth, and the life; no one comes to the Father, but by me" (John 14:6).

Thus, the Spirit of truth is a vital, and not mainly an intellectual, source of guidance. It is not to be identified with correct theologies in any manner that would give absolute authority to one, and only one, as authenticated by the Holy Spirit. Too much of human frailty enters into the quest. Yet, on the other hand, it is a mistake to divorce the Holy Spirit from man's continuing search for Christian truth. Pastor John Robinson was right when he told the pilgrims departing from Leyden that "the Lord has more truth yet to break forth out of his holy Word." In its discovery the Holy Spirit, attuning the seeker to the Spirit of Christ, is an indispensable aid.

The Spirit of truth is epitomized in the Methodist creed that was quoted in our first chapter:

We believe in the Holy Spirit as the divine presence in our lives, whereby we are kept in perpetual remembrance of the truth of Christ, and find strength and help in time of need.

At the Last Supper the promise is given equally of disclosure of truth and of "strength and help in time of need." Whether that time of need be loneliness, uncertainty of the future, confusion and chaos, sorrow or sin, the Counselor who is also the Comforter will be there. There is a marvelous conjunction of the promise of instruction in truth with the comfort of inner spiritual peace in the words:

"These things I have spoken to you, while I am still with you. But the Counselor, the Holy Spirit, whom the Father will send in my name, he will teach you all things, and bring to your remembrance all that I have said to you. Peace I leave with you; my peace I give to you; not as the world gives do I give to you. Let not your hearts be troubled, neither let them be afraid." (John 14:25-27.)

This instruction in truth and the promised peace are gifts, immeasurable gifts. Yet they do not come without commensurate demands. "If you love me, you will keep my commandments. . . . By this my Father is glorified, that you bear much fruit, and so prove to be my disciples. . . . This is my commandment, that you love one another as I have loved you"

79

(John 14:15; 15:8, 12). In our Lord's promise of the Holy Spirit, there is no "cheap grace"! [4]

Thus, the coming Holy Spirit is inseparably linked with the Jesus of history, and with the living Christ that is to be present with his followers after the resurrection. The thought of John is not quite identical with that of Paul. We have noted that Paul does not hesitate to merge the identity of God, Christ, and the Spirit in the inclusive concept of "the Lord," while to John the Spirit will come to take the place of the Christ known to his disciples upon earth. Yet nearly everything said of the coming of the Spirit is said of Christ's abiding presence. The convergence appears also in the fact that the emphasis in John is thoroughly ethical with the most rigorous demand and the finest fruit of the Spirit in love. Substitute "the mind of Christ" for "the Spirit of truth," and the identity is almost complete.

A more radical disparity in the record appears at another point. When did the Holy Spirit come? According to Luke in Acts, at Pentecost. According to John, at the post-Resurrection appearance recorded in 20:19-23. Here we are told that Jesus appeared among his disciples, blessed them, breathed on them, and said, "Receive the Holy Spirit. If you forgive the sins of any, they are forgiven; if you retain the sins of any, they are retained." This is a controversial passage, and most Protestants prefer the account in Acts.

Enough has been said to indicate the heights to which an understanding of the Holy Spirit had come by the time the

[4] A term used by Dietrich Bonhoeffer in *The Cost of Discipleship*, trans. R. H. Fuller (New York: Macmillan Co., 1960), in repudiation of the idea that justification by faith demands nothing of the recipient of God's grace.

Fourth Gospel was written. Echoing but not simply repeating the emphasis of Paul in the early years of the Church, the Last Supper discourse presents in the most tender and persuasive way the work of the Holy Spirit. What is accented is the continuity of the Holy Spirit with the Jesus who as the Son of God lived and died and rose again, and hence the guidance of the mind and the strengthening of the soul in faith and love. This is what the Holy Spirit has been doing through all the centuries to the present, and it is the very heart and groundwork of Christian faith. The doctrine of the Trinity was yet to be developed, but its makings were all there.

V

THE WORK
OF
THE HOLY SPIRIT

In the preceding chapters, and particularly in the three devoted to a biblical survey, we have had occasion repeatedly to note the effects of the Spirit in human life. There has been no systematic discussion of these effects, but it is impossible to consider properly what the Holy Spirit *is* without recognition of what the Spirit *does*. This is inevitable, for the Holy Spirit is no inert entity or metaphysical essence, but the living God himself as he imparts grace and power to the human spirit.

In the chapter which follows this one, we shall move into a difficult, but from a Christian standpoint an unavoidable, question, the doctrine of the Trinity. There we shall discover that the Trinity makes sense if it is grounded in Christian experience. If it is not, the problems multiply until irrationality breeds despair.

The present chapter, standing midway between the biblical survey and the theological issue soon to be examined, has a dual purpose. It aims to lay further groundwork for the declaration that the Trinity makes sense if it is rooted in

Christian experience. Further than that, it aims to suggest from a biblical base how the works of the Spirit, manifold but discernible as certain continuing types, are vitally relevant to life at all times. Far from being simply an historical legacy from long ago, the Holy Spirit is still "God present and God acting."

Where shall we begin? As we saw in noting Paul's contributions, he recognized that the work of the Holy Spirit relates to the whole of life. The whole of life is many-sided, and thus every angle is related to every other. Yet there can be no system without a beginning somewhere, and this involves a selection of categories and their arrangement in a sequence.

The rubrics I shall adopt are historical and biblical, but they are also contemporary in meaning if not in terminology. Let us, then, think of the work of the Holy Spirit as the Life-giver, as Source of power, as Sanctifier, and as Revealer of truth.

1. AS THE GIVER OF LIFE

In the Nicene Creed, repeated times without number in services of Christian worship since the end of the fourth century of our era, stand the words, "I believe in the Holy Ghost, the Lord, the giver of life." That the Holy Spirit is the Lord, even though not the only manifestation of the Lord, is clearly evident in the New Testament and especially in the words of both Paul and John. But what does it mean to say that he is also the giver of life?

To retrace some ground, though from a new perspective, even before the Old Testament and its people and times emerged, there was a belief in spirit as the giver of everything important. Whether as many spirits in animism, as *mana* in a semi-pantheistic monism, or personalized in some such fashion as in Longfellow's

> Gitche Manito, the mighty,
> The Great Spirit, the creator,[1]

both nature and human life were more than themselves, and owed their existence to a Power beyond themselves. This mysterious Power—this "something more"—was spirit, not material substance, and Spirit was the life-giver.

This primitive faith was, of course, transcended in both Hebrew and Christian thought. It must be affirmed beyond possible misunderstanding that origins do not determine or define the subsequent stages of development. A higher stage was reached when in the words of the Jahwist writer (the "J" narrative of creation) we find in Genesis 2:7, "Then the Lord God formed man of dust from the ground, and breathed into his nostrils the breath of life; and man became a living being." Still later the author of the priestly, post-exilic story of creation suggests that the Spirit of God not only gives life to man but order to nature, "The earth was without form and void, and darkness was upon the face of the deep; and the Spirit of God was moving over the face of the waters" (Gen. 1:2).

It would not be profitable to restate here all that was said in chapter two about the work of the Spirit as it is found in the Old Testament. However, Ezekiel's vision of the revivification in the valley of dry bones is especially pertinent. Israel was alive biologically; it was almost dead spiritually. This

---

[1] From Part One of Longfellow's *Hiawatha*.

makes the similarity between this situation in the sixth century B.C. and our own times striking, and this prophetic writing very relevant. Professor F. W. Dillistone says in this connection:

The importance of this vision for our investigation lies in the fact that we find here a new conception of the nature of life. Life is not only something physical or natural, for the exiles were still alive in that respect. But they were without God and without hope in the world. Cut off from a vital relationship with God they were as good as dead. But now it is the Spirit who is the giver of a new kind of life: life in relationship with God and with one another (v. 22), life that is holy and pure (v. 23), life that is peaceful and fruitful (v. 26), life that is suffused with the presence and blessing of God Himself (v. 27.) Here then we have a new vision of what renewed and regenerated life may be.[2]

Not until the coming of Christ did this vision find fulfillment. Then it was not the nation, but individuals, that "came alive" with a great new faith and hope. This occurred again and again as Jesus brought healing, cleansing, and renewal of life to those whose lives he touched. We have seen that this was a major note in the coming of the Holy Spirit at Pentecost. Such new life in the Spirit is evidenced in the courage to witness to the faith and to spread the gospel to ever-widening areas that shines through the pages of the book of Acts and Paul's letters. For Paul such new life in the Spirit begins, continues, and ends in the living Christ, and his major message is its availability through God's grace to any who will claim it in penitence, faith, and love.

[2] In *The Holy Spirit in the Life of Today* (Philadelphia: Westminster Press, 1957), pp. 41 f. The verse references are to Ezekiel 37.

So it is in John's Gospel. In the Prologue we are at once given assurance of the life-giving power of the Word, "In him was life, and the life was the light of men" (vs. 4). The Gospel as a whole witnesses to the possibility of the new birth and new life in the Son. It closes with the coming of the Spirit to continue the work of the Son in imparting eternal life to those who will believe in him and live in love with one another.[3]

The difference such new life makes is not defined for us, point by point, in the Bible. Yet it is indicated clearly enough at many points. More basic than any specific injunction or promise of change is the transformation of motive, of orientation, of outlook on life, of sources of reliance, of goals of endeavor—in short of the human spirit as it lives in relation to God and man. It is no exaggeration to say that when this occurs, whether suddenly or gradually, at the depths of one's being "it makes all the difference in the world." And, were we to have a society of such transformed spirits, it could make a vast difference *to* the world.

Thus far, we have thought of the Holy Spirit as life-giver to the individual. This, indeed, is what the Bible for the most part does. Yet the work of the Spirit is by no means limited to solitary selves, or even to persons in their immediate, face-to-face relations.

[3] As was indicated in the preceding chapter, the *promise* of the Spirit is much more dominant in John's Gospel than is the brief account of the Spirit's coming. The Roman Catholic Church includes in its ordination service the post-resurrection words, "Receive the Holy Spirit," and finds authority for its priesthood in the ensuing promise, "If you forgive the sins of any, they are forgiven; if you retain the sins of any, they are retained" (John 20:22, 23). These words probably reflect in some degree Matt. 16:19.

The Church came into being through the life-giving work of the Holy Spirit. That is what Pentecost is all about. Probably not all of the initial 120 Christians in that company, and certainly not all of the ensuing 3000, knew each other by face and name. Yet all were quickened to new life both individually and in their corporate relations, and the Church was born.

So it has remained to the present insofar as the Church has been Christ-centered, life-renewing in its service, and renewed in its own life as changes have taken place from age to age. There have been arid stretches, and as institutions took shape and form tended to replace spirit, the glow of Pentecost faded. Administrators replaced prophets, and the sacraments became functional elements in ecclesiastical control. Yet never wholly, and the institutions and sacraments may themselves be regarded as the vehicle of the Holy Spirit to the extent that they are genuine channels of grace. Without them the Church, if it continued to exist, would be much weakened in its endeavors for the glory of God and the service of the world.

There is much talk today of the sterility of the Church, of its being out of touch with the modern world, of its need of change. There is truth in these charges, though they are often exaggerated, and we must look at them further in a later chapter. Yet two things must here be said; first, that the Holy Spirit has continued to be the life-giver of the Church through nearly twenty centuries and, second, that in times of special need, as in the days of the Reformation and the denominational divisions of the present, the Spirit has quickened the Church to new vitality and a renewed sense of its mission.

Roman Catholics and Protestants may continue to differ,

as they have in the past, on the proper interpretation of the words of Jesus in Matthew 16:18, "On this rock I will build my church, and the powers of death shall not prevail against it." Yet on the reality and activity of the Holy Spirit there is great agreement. Furthermore, the Christian who believes that the Church must go forward, not by its wealth, prestige, or clever adaptation to the secular world but by the power of the Spirit, will scarcely doubt the realism of the promise that "the powers of death shall not prevail against it."

Some would stop at this point, and regard the life-giving work of the Holy Spirit as limited to the Christian experience of the individual believer and the corporate fellowship of the Church. Here we must be careful in our use of terms. We have seen that the Holy Spirit, as two words with one meaning, is found only in the New Testament, and as a designation for the living Christ still present in the lives of his followers, it is limited to a Christian context. Nevertheless, the Holy Spirit is the Spirit of God, and the divine Creator Spirit is not thus limited. The "living God who made the heaven and the earth and the sea and all that is in them . . . did not leave himself without witness" (Acts 14:15-17) among any people.

From this far-reaching fact it is legitimate to infer that the Spirit of God is present in the spiritual strivings, insights, and achievements of people who seek him through other paths than the Christian. Furthermore, he is present in the life-giving forces of nature. The passage just quoted continues with evidence of this, "For he did good and gave you from heaven rains and fruitful seasons, satisfying your hearts with food and gladness" (vs. 17). Need we hesitate to say that the Spirit is present and active in man's utilization of these gifts for human good? If we may, then the life-giving eternal Spirit is present also in man's eternal quest for goodness, truth, and beauty; for government "with liberty and justice for all"; for spiritual foundations in other high religions. This is not to say that any of these channels of the Spirit can be a substitute for the Christian way; it is to say that "God is greater than our hearts" (I John 3:20), and it is unbecoming for us to fence in the life-giving work of his Spirit.

An ancient prayer, spoken in services of worship for many centuries and still in use in the more liturgical churches, is *"Veni, Creator Spiritus!"* *"Come, Creator Spirit!"* This may well be our prayer today.

2. AS SOURCE OF POWER

If there is one thing that all persons may be said to possess, it is a desire for power. Even the ever-present fact of human sin is not more pervasive, for it is in the longing for or the exercise of power to be, to do, or to have what one wants, regardless of obligation to God or man, that the sinning lies.

There are, of course, many kinds of power. As power to survive, the instinctual urge to self-preservation is shared with man by the animal world, and to this is linked in varying degrees the power to possess and to dominate. It characterizes nations, races, economic, cultural, and even ecclesiastical groups as well as individuals. No society could exist without it, yet from this fact stem some of the greatest perversions of justice. Obviously, the Holy Spirit may not be regarded as the source of the manifold perversions of power which are visible to anyone who reads his newspaper or listens to the radio or television.

It is power of a different sort, centering in self-mastery, concern for others, and obedience to the divine will that the Holy Spirit imparts. It is epitomized in the power of love and the reconciliation of man to God and to one another through love. Yet the power of the Spirit is no vague emotion dignified with the name of love; it is a dynamic, energizing force.

To glance again at the biblical sources, wherever the Spirit of God appears in the Old Testament there is an imparting of power, whether of physical strength to Samson, ecstatic utterance to the early bands of prophets, inspiration to the great prophets, or revivification to Israel. In the Gospels the Holy Spirit is to come upon Mary by the power of the Most High (Luke 1:35); Jesus returns from the wilderness temptation in the power of the Spirit (Luke 4:14); he undertakes his life's mission in the conviction that the Spirit of the Lord is upon him (vs. 18). Nowhere in the Gospels is the relation between the Holy Spirit and the earthly ministry of Jesus more clearly stated than in Peter's words to Cornelius in the tenth chapter of Acts, "You know . . . how God anointed Jesus of Nazareth with the Holy Spirit and with power; how he went about doing good and healing all that were oppressed by the devil, for God was with him" (Acts 10:36-38).

It is, of course, in the book of Acts and in the letters that one sees the tremendous increments of power that came into the lives of ordinary persons when they were Spirit-filled and Spirit-led. It is significant that in the post-resurrection promise of the coming of the Holy Spirit as this is recorded in Acts, power is the one specific gift mentioned (Acts 1:8). This gift was bountifully imparted and gloriously used. The records of courage under difficulty, forthright and inspired witness in speech, and fidelity in Christian living under tremendous odds ought never to leave us unmoved. Further healings of the infirmities of the body are recorded, but most of all, the healing power of the Spirit. Like a cleansing wind—to revert to the original meaning of the term—the Holy Spirit blows away the mists and impurities of the human spirit to give new life and new power.

We shall be looking in the next section at some of the gifts and graces that are the fruit of such a transformation. We must conclude this one with a look at a form of power of which Paul makes a great deal; namely, freedom.

Freedom does not mean unrestricted liberty, whether in government, community patterns of behavior, the family, or anywhere else. Attempts to have freedom without any restraint soon run into anarchy, and this precipitates tyranny both in external control and in chaotic inner pressures. This is a primary source of wreckage both in social groups and individual personalities. As surely as traffic signals must be obeyed to avoid catastrophe along the highways, so must disciplines prevail in human relations.

Yet such disciplines, imposed from without, may themselves seem impossible hurdles. This is the way Paul felt about the Law, which he found himself unable to keep. The truly effective disciplines must be accepted from within, and with the assurance of understanding love, companionship, and help. Then a new freedom emerges.

It was this emancipation of spirit that Paul found in Christ through the Holy Spirit. Thereafter he did not feel himself a slave to other men or to old traditions, but to Christ alone. Obligations there still were, more binding than before, but they were obligations accepted with a new zest. They could be accepted seriously but joyously, by men who found themselves no longer slaves to legalism or to passion but sons of God.

Such triumphant living appears repeatedly in Paul's writing and especially in his letter to the Galatian church. Its fifth chapter opens on the note of assurance and challenge, "For freedom Christ has set us free; stand fast therefore, and do not submit again to a yoke of slavery" (vs. 1). It ends with the moral injunction, "If we live by the Spirit, let us also walk by the Spirit. Let us have no self-conceit, no provoking of one another, no envy of one another" (vss. 25-26).

Familiar as we are today with the disorders that send people to psychiatrists and mental hospitals, with family quarrels terminating in broken homes, with bitter strife between racial, economic, and national groups, who can say that such counsel is irrelevant to the times? If such freedom is possible through ordered and disciplined living in the power of the Spirit, we had better find it!

3. AS SANCTIFIER

Sanctification with its correlative term "holiness," as applied to Christian experience, is in bad odor today. Those of an older generation (and possibly not so old) who have heard those of the "holiness" sects talk about their "entire sanctification," claiming a self-righteous superiority in the victory over sin which others fail to see manifest in their living, will have no truck with either term. Recent theology with its stress on the holiness of God but the sinfulness and unworthiness of man moves in the same direction. If we add to "sanctification" and "holiness" a third term, "Christian perfection," the rout is apt to be complete.

With the rejection of what these terms are commonly taken to mean, I have great sympathy. However sincere the belief that one has reached the point of no return in his sinning, sin remains, and the Christian must fight an ongoing battle with it. To repent, to ask forgiveness of God and usually of the human person sinned against, and to go forward humbly by God's grace, is the continuing experience of the Christian.

Yet in a deeper sense, the Holy Spirit remains the Sanctifier that the Christian tradition has long conceived him to be. The Latin "sanctus" is the English "holy," and the Holy Spirit does impart what John Wesley called "scriptural holiness." God's design in raising up the people called Methodists, he said, was not to form a new sect but "to reform the nation, particularly the Church, and to spread scriptural holiness over the land." It need hardly be said that this task is not the exclusive prerogative of Methodists.

Such scriptural holiness with the Christian perfection which is its goal would arouse less confusion and dissent if it were understood to mean growth in Christian experience and in moral victory through Christ. It means, in short, "growing in grace," and there is no finer statement of its meaning than in the injunction found in II Peter 3:18, "But grow in the grace and knowledge of our Lord and Savior Jesus Christ. To him be the glory both now and to the day of eternity." The New English Bible further accents Christian maturity by suggesting an alternative reading, "But grow up, by the grace of our Lord and Savior Jesus Christ, and by knowing him."

John Wesley may have had more confidence in the possibility of Christian perfection, or of being "made perfect in love in this life," [4] than do most Christians today. Yet what he was above all concerned about was the actual difference it makes to become a Christian and to continue going forward in the Christian way. And on this point, and on the work of the Holy Spirit in the daily demands of Christian living, the New Testament is completely clear.

Note, for example, some words of Paul to the Corinthian church. They were by no means perfect people, as his numerous moral injunctions to these and the other early Christians indicate. Yet they were different from their former selves because a new spirit and mode of living had come into their lives through the grace of God in Christ, mediated to them through the Holy Spirit. Let us hear him speak to them and to our own times:

Do you not know that the unrighteous will not inherit the kingdom of God? Do not be deceived; neither the immoral, nor idolaters, nor adulterers, nor homosexuals, nor thieves, nor the greedy, nor drunkards, nor revilers, nor robbers will inherit the kingdom of God. And such were some of you. But you were washed, you were sanctified, you were justified in the name of the Lord Jesus Christ and in the Spirit of our God. (I Cor. 6:9-11.)

[4] Every Methodist minister upon becoming a full member of a conference is still asked these questions formulated by John Wesley:
    (1) Have you faith in Christ?
    (2) Are you going on to perfection?
    (3) Do you expect to be made perfect in love in this life?
    (4) Are you earnestly striving after it?
The questions dealing with Christian perfection may be and often are reinterpreted to stress the seriousness of one's Christian calling, but respect for tradition has thus far prevented their removal.

It would be difficult to find a more apt list of the types of moral perversion prevalent both in Paul's day and in ours. Yet before we fix attention unduly on the perversions in a pharisaic spirit, it is essential to remember that the Holy Spirit comes both to such overt transgressors and to conventionally moral people to challenge, purify, and upbuild us "through the name of the Lord Jesus and the Spirit of our God" (vs. 11, NEB). This has always happened where Christian witness has been vital; it happens today.

Since in traditional terminology a sharp distinction is sometimes drawn between justification and sanctification, a further word at this point may be in order. There is certainly a difference between the initial act of decision for Christ, which may be accompanied by a great emotional glow though it need not be, and the humdrum and difficult processes of daily Christian living. Yet there is no absolute line of demarcation. What the Holy Spirit does in bringing us to Christian commitment, whether suddenly or gradually, is also what the Holy Spirit does in the years of growth to greater Christian maturity. What is different is that "every one to whom much is given, of him will much be required" (Luke 12:48). As the gifts and the requirements increase, so does the sense of the undergirding presence and power of the Holy Spirit. There may be less of an ecstatic glow about it; what matters is that the light still shines and the fire burns.

The New Testament abounds in passages which indicate the difference the Holy Spirit makes in the life of the Christian. Perhaps the greatest, and certainly the most familiar, is "the more excellent way" set forth in I Corinthians 13. Yet for a summary of the gifts and graces imparted by the Spirit, nothing excels Galatians 5:22: "But the fruit of the Spirit is love, joy, peace, patience, kindness, goodness, faithfulness, gentleness, self-control; against such there is no law." Nor, we may add, is there any insuperable barrier to such fruit in those who will let the Spirit have his way within us.

4. AS REVEALER OF TRUTH

One cannot read the account of the promise of the coming of the Holy Spirit as found in the Last Supper discourse in John's Gospel without discovering the prominence given to the work of the Holy Spirit as the revealer of truth. Yet it it is truth projected forward from the revelation already given in Christ. In the words Jesus is quoted as speaking to his disciples the Counselor, the Holy Spirit, will "bring to your remembrance all that I have said to you" (14:26); the Counselor "will bear witness to me" (15:26); the Spirit of truth "will take what is mine and declare it to you" (16:14). It is clear that to the author of this Gospel the Spirit's revelation of truth was to be no independent witness dissociated from the truth already disclosed. Yet it is equally clear that the entire mood of these passages is open-ended and oriented toward the future. This is implied throughout but epitomized in the words, "I have yet many things to say to you, but you cannot bear them now. When the Spirit of truth comes, he will guide you into all the truth" (16:12-13).

This was the mood of the early church. We are told repeatedly that human wisdom is not sufficient, for "no one comprehends the thoughts of God except the Spirit of God" (I Cor. 2:11). In a magnificent passage in First Corinthians Paul speaks with glowing fervor both of "the deep things of God" and of our knowledge of them only through the Spirit:

Eye hath not seen, nor ear heard, neither have entered into the heart of man, the things which God hath prepared for them that love him.

But God hath revealed them unto us by his Spirit: for the Spirit searcheth all things, yea, the deep things of God. (I Cor. 2:9-10, KJV.)

To Paul the Spirit is the only valid authority for imparting or receiving the message of the gospel, for the gifts of the Spirit of God must be spiritually discerned (vss. 13, 14). Yet the Spirit is not something that comes in a vacuum, or without antecedent. No man is wise enough to know the mind of the Lord, transcendent as it is to human wisdom. But we are not left without knowledge, for "we have the mind of Christ" (vs. 16).

The term "inspiration" is often bandied about today, whether in reference to the Bible or to some kind of human experience which may or may not be religious. Without attempting to give an extended analysis of its meaning it may be pointed out that there is a direct connection between the Holy Spirit and a Christian understanding of inspiration. In the field of Christian faith and life, the possibility of new insights depends not only on long and rigorous search but on the illumination of the Spirit. In fact, the word inspiration means "inbreathing"—a cognate term to the original meaning of "spirit." This readily suggests that the breath of God continues to blow upon the human spirit from the supreme and decisive revelation in God's Son.

The conviction that the Holy Spirit continues to impart to the receptive human spirit fresh discoveries of Christian truth has had great consequences in the history of the Church. The movement has not always been forward, for ecclesiastical dogma and practice has for long periods fenced in the authority of the Spirit, not denying its existence but claiming superior authority. Biblical literalism has often been an inhibiting force. Excesses beyond reason among those who claimed the authority of the Spirit have led to its rejection of curtailment. Yet after seasons of stagnation in the churches, new Spirit-led movements have emerged to quicken them to new vitality.

This appears to be an ever-repeated process. After periods of recession the Holy Spirit has guided and empowered Christian life and thought toward a more vital discovery and proclamation of the gospel. This has usually been accompanied by a fuller service to humanity in the spirit of Christ. Within recent years the currents of change under the guidance of the Spirit appear to be moving toward a closer unity within the churches. This is true in both the non-Roman and Roman Catholic ecumenical movements with their growing interchange of fellowship and understanding.

The possibility of the discovery of new truth and a fresh understanding of the will of God amid changing circumstances is a great boon. Yet it is beset with perils. No communication is given except to and through human minds, and these are always susceptible to sin and error. Ever in the offing is the danger lest human presumption replace divine leading. That this can happen unconsciously even in sincere Christians, and perhaps most often in persons of such inflexible conviction that a sense of dogmatic certainty replaces humble quest, should put us all on guard.

To know when we are hearing the voice of the Holy Spirit, and when we are listening to our own unhallowed subconscious impulses, is not an easy matter. There are indices and channels of discovery in an unbiased and comprehensive survey of the total situation, in corporate worship that is deep and genuine, in interchange of thought with other wise and well-grounded Christians, in prayer and commitment that carries with it a willingness to go where the Spirit leads. Yet there is one safeguard that is indispensable to all others. It is what Paul calls the mind of Christ. Whatever carries forward our understanding of God and of his will as this has been revealed to us in Jesus *is* the work of the Holy Spirit; all else is suspect.

Enough has been said to indicate the inseparable connection both in the New Testament and in living experience of God the Father, Jesus Christ the Son, and the Holy Spirit. But how did the three become one in the doctrine of the Trinity? This must be our next inquiry.

VI

THE DOCTRINE
OF
THE TRINITY

We have now traced the course of the Holy Spirit in biblical thought from its earliest stages, in a windlike supernatural power that enabled those on whom it came to do remarkable and even fantastic things, to its climax in the thought of Paul and the author of the Fourth Gospel. In this process we have seen the Spirit conceived as becoming increasingly ethical, personal, and intimately related to Jesus Christ. In brief, the Spirit of God becomes in the New Testament Holy Spirit, and the Holy Spirit becomes the risen and living Christ. Jesus, the Son of God incarnate within the stream of history, dies and returns to the Father; the Holy Spirit as Comforter, Counselor, Advocate, Life-giver, Christ here and now, is present with his followers throughout all time.

Thus far, there is no *doctrine* of the Trinity. Yet there are many intimations that God is to be thought of as Father, Son, and Holy Spirit, and not as three gods but one. These intimations become most concrete in the baptismal formula of Matthew 28:19 and the apostolic benediction of Second Corinthians 13:14, but the passages cited in the preceding chapters have made it clear that the identification, or at least the close conjunction, of these three terms appears repeatedly in the New Testament writings.

The steps by which these intimations grew into a doctrine are complex and long-drawn-out. To trace them with any adequacy would require a book in itself, and for the reader to follow them would presuppose a rather extensive knowledge of early church history. All we shall attempt, therefore, in this chapter is to show why the Trinity became a doctrine and to indicate the principal steps of its development into an accepted article of the Christian creeds.

1. THE FOUNDATIONS IN EXPERIENCE

Many persons if asked today what they mean by the Holy Spirit would reply, "The third person of the Trinity." The Christians of the first century would have given no such reply. Yet they believed profoundly in the Holy Spirit who had transformed their lives and was guiding and strengthening them in their daily living. On this basis, and this only, the doctrine could take shape, foreshadowed first in the ritual of Christian baptism and later wrought into the creeds.

In our time we cannot hope to apprehend the Trinity as a doctrine, or see in it anything but a curious blending of three gods into one, unless we too get at its meaning through experience. It is not impossible to think of it in a way that makes sense. It is not at bottom irrational, though some forms are in which it has been held. Yet it is not primarily logical deduction, or even a long tradition in the Church, but Christian experience which commends it to us. Had not the Trinity been formulated in the early centuries, something else to fulfill the same purpose would have needed to be.

This primary basis in experience has been suggested in the previous chapters and it appears, long before there was a doctrine of the Trinity, in numerous of Paul's statements. For example, "God has sent the Spirit of his Son into our hearts" (Gal. 4:6). He speaks movingly of the illumination of the Holy Spirit as he writes, "God's love has been poured into our hearts through the Holy Spirit which has been given to us" (Rom. 5:5) and in a similar vein of "the light of the knowledge of the glory of God in the face of Christ" (II Cor. 4:6). The basic foundation of belief in experience is affirmed categorically in the words, "No one can say 'Jesus is Lord' except by the Holy Spirit" (I Cor. 12:3).

Yet we do not need to go back to Paul to discover this truth. The twin perils which have long beset Christian faith from the standpoint of belief in the Trinity are tritheism and what is now termed unitarianism. Although the theologians of the early centuries of the Christian Church envisaged the issues somewhat differently, as we must note in a later section, these are the two main pitfalls which a trinitarian faith must guard against. Those who take literally the historic affirmation of "God in three persons, blessed Trinity" without understanding what this means are prone unconsciously to fall into the worship of three gods. In revulsion from such a conclusion, not only the followers of Mohammed but the contemporary exponents of Jewish monotheism, Christian Unitarianism,[1] and many humanists who admire

---

[1] The question is often asked, "Are Unitarians Christians?" I do not favor excluding from the Christian fellowship those who believe in and worship the God of Jesus and who "profess and call themselves Christians." Neither do I rule out the tritheists!

the teachings of Jesus but would hesitate to say "Jesus is Lord," reject outright the Christian doctrine of the Trinity.

What this means is that the doctrine of the Trinity rests centrally on the Incarnation. If Jesus was only a prophet, an ethical teacher, a religious genius, or a saint, his inspiration through the Spirit of God in the Old Testament sense might still be believed in. Yet there would be no Holy Spirit in the New Testament context, and no need of a doctrine of the Trinity. What the early creed makers were attempting to do was to preserve the faith of Christians in a unique incarnation of God in Jesus Christ his Son, and the continuity of Jesus of Nazareth in some sense with the experienced presence of the Holy Spirit. This is still our task, though we tend to approach it differently.

This relation of doctrine to experience is summarized thus by H. Wheeler Robinson:

The contribution of the New Testament towards a doctrine of the Godhead is thus seen to be historical and experiential rather than theological. All that we are entitled to say is that both in Jesus Christ and in that inner appropriation of Him ascribed to the work of the Spirit the Christians were conscious that God was present with them, and so felt the importance of this Presence as essential to the experience of salvation, that they often named these distinguished, though not separated, activities side by side with the activity of God, because in fact they were essential to the Christian experience of the presence of God.[2]

He concludes further that the *issues* raised for us by the doctrine of the Trinity are present in the New Testament,

[2] *The Christian Experience of the Holy Spirit*, pp. 234 f.

while the doctrine itself is not. This puts the matter so aptly that we may now look at what the early creed makers were trying not only to affirm but to protect the gospel from falling into.

2. PROTECTION FROM PITFALLS

In view of the dramatic change in the modes of worship and practice in Christ's followers after the resurrection, it could easily have been assumed that a new mystery cult had appeared. The Graeco-Roman world was full of such cults which in one way or another offered salvation. In some of them, indeed, there were triads of deities—a fact which has led some persons to assume that the Christian Trinity simply copied current practice. In Egyptian religion there was the worship of Osiris, Isis, and Horus—Father, Mother, and Son. There was the Phrygian Cybele, who became the Roman Magna Mater, and her son Attis whom she brought back from the dead. Most vigorous of all the rivals of Christianity was the religion of Mithra, which appealed particularly to the Roman soldiers. Only men were initiated into the Mithra mysteries, and the fact that ruins of the temples of the Great Mother are found near those of Mithra has led to the supposition that their women worshiped Cybele and Attis.

How much the adherents of these faiths actually believed in the existence of these mythological figures it is difficult to say. Considering the power of tradition and the credulity of the human spirit, they probably did. However, with the Christians there was no uncertainty about the historical existence of their Lord! Some had known him in his brief ministry upon earth. When those who "knew him in the flesh knew him no more," as was the case during the beginnings of creedal formulations in the second to fourth centuries, they had an indisputable witness, not only in memories handed down and in written records but in the Christian fellowship.

The true historicity of the revelation of God in human form in Jesus Christ had to be protected at all costs. The first heresy to be combatted by the Church was docetism, an aspect of Gnosticism, which did not deny that Jesus had lived, but did question his full humanity. As a divine being he had only *appeared* to be human, according to this view, and had seemed to suffer agony and death upon the cross without really doing so. Had this been allowed to stand, there would have been no incarnation. Hence, the reiteration in the Apostles' Creed of the phrases that stress his humanity in conjunction with his Sonship—conceived, born, suffered, was crucified, dead, and buried.

Except as the Sonship of Jesus was attested by his miraculous conception, all this could be said without reference to the Holy Spirit. No description or amplification seemed necessary. The brevity of the simple statement, "I believe in the Holy Spirit," (or Holy Ghost) as it stands in the Apostles' Creed to the present is evidence that no elaboration was thought to be needed. However, that it appears at all is indirectly a witness to the reality of the incarnation as both historical and contemporary fact. Jesus was born, suffered, died, rose again, returned to God the Father, will come again. Meanwhile, he who said, "Lo, I am with you always, to the close of the age" (Matt. 28:20), is with his followers as Holy Spirit. This last implication is not spelled out, but it is

needed both to complete what comes before this third affirmation of the creed and to prepare the way for the historical
and eschatological notes that follow it.

A second danger to be guarded against was a too exclusive
objectivity or subjectivity. The reality of the incarnation preserved the objectivity of God's revelation and of God's saving
work for sinful humanity. Yet God speaks to and works in and
with individual persons. Salvation is a Person to person
encounter. And how does God come into the life of the
individual? The answer is the living Christ or the Holy Spirit
—one may use either term. It is God present and God acting
where we are that preserves the subjective aspect of the
divine-human encounter without losing its objectivity. Therefore, to deal theologically with the Holy Spirit within the
Trinity is to be concerned about safeguarding the Christian's
personal participation in God's revelation.

This is true in our experience quite apart from theological
analysis. If we were to think solely of God as Creator and
Sustainer of the universe, he would be a God "out there."
It is quite possible to study the life and teachings of Jesus,
admire him greatly, and even to believe theoretically in his
divinity, without becoming a Christian. The work of the Holy
Spirit when examined as a psychological phenomenon may
be interesting and enlightening, but this is unlikely to make
much difference in one's motivations or sources of strength.
Thus far, the elements of the Trinity are viewed as objects,
without personal involvement. It is when these three approaches to deity are brought together in a living commitment that the Christian's subjective, yet objective, participation in God's threefold revelation takes place.

It is not to be assumed that the early formulators of the

creeds looked at this matter from exactly our standpoint. They did not have to be concerned about humanism, ethical relativism, depth psychology or the projection of the ego, though there were "strange gods" and expressions of religious indifference in plentiful supply. Nevertheless, by a deep-going logic of the spirit they saw that Father, Son, and Holy Spirit belonged together as one God, not only in the baptismal formula but in life. Hence, they did not hesitate to put them together in the doctrine of the Trinity.

Another pitfall to be avoided was an exaggerated dualism. Marcion in the second century saw the world as full of evil, and saw no way to amalgamate the Creator God of the Old Testament with the Redeemer God of Jesus. Accordingly, he rejected the Old Testament outright. As a result, Tertullian and others felt impelled to assert the unity of the God who creates and the God who redeems. To this assertion was linked the unity in differentiation of Father, Son, and Spirit, *una substantia, tres personae,* of which we must say more presently. Somewhat curiously, the Church owes its first formation of a canon of the New Testament Scriptures to this heretic, for Marcion, a great admirer of Paul, brought together ten of Paul's letters and portions of the Gospel of Luke as a substitute for the rejected Old Testament.

Two centuries later another form of dualism, that of Arius, precipitated the controversy that brought together the Nicene Council and resulted in a long step toward the formulation of the Trinity. Affirming the existence of one God, utterly transcendent, he believed also that an intermediate being, the Logos or Christ, connected this God with the created world. Yet this intermediate deity, created by the Father, was subordinate to the Father and neither fully God nor fully man.

This the orthodox Christian fathers could not accept, and the Nicene affirmation of faith was the consequence.

The opposite extreme of dualism was an exaggerated monism, or immanentism, which readily slips over into pantheism. Nature cults of the life-giving forces, the all-pervasive Logos of Stoic thought, various forms of mysticism, and the Spirit-possession of the Montanists all tended in this direction. This seems to be a persistent tendency of human nature, for in present-day Christianity there is more than a little of the worship of God in nature which tends to exalt nature more than God. One often hears talk of being "one with the Infinite," and of the identification of God with the "divine spark" in every man. This was not in the early centuries (nor is it now) authentic Christianity, and the Trinity is needed as a safeguard against it.[3]

3. HOW THE TRINITY GREW

The earliest explicit statement, as has been noted, was the formula of baptism in the threefold name (Matt. 28:19). Elsewhere in the New Testament baptism was in the name of Jesus (Acts 2:38; 8:16; 10:48; 19:5) but before the end of the first century the triadic form was being used. As today it is the familiar phrases used in church worship that tend to shape the theology of the worshipers, so it was in that period.

The next step is the expansion of this formula into the Old Roman symbol in the second century, which was eventually to grow into the Apostles' Creed. Probably under the influ-

[3] This does not exclude the possibility that Christian mystics may also be Trinitarians. It is against the substitution of such forms of immanentism for the Incarnation that the Trinity is a safeguard.

ence of Irenaeus between 175 and 200, and certainly by the time of Tertullian in the late second century, the original brief statement had become considerably amplified, to read as follows:

I believe in God Father Almighty; and in Christ Jesus his Son, who was born of Mary the Virgin, was crucified under Pontius Pilate and buried, on the third day arose from the dead, ascended into heaven, sitteth at the right hand of the Father, whence he cometh to judge living and dead; and in Holy Spirit, resurrection of flesh.

This is the form cited by A. C. McGiffert,[4] though other texts give minor variants. He contends that it was framed in opposition to Marcion's form of Gnosticism, and that this polemical purpose is the reason why it contains no reference to such vital elements of Christian faith as "the kingdom of God, the Messiahship of Jesus, his fulfillment of prophecy, his divinity, his preexistence, his baptism, his teaching, his revelation of God's will and truth, his sinlessness, his works of mercy and power, his victory over demons, the purpose of his death." [5]

Some other scholars are less inclined to regard this earliest version of the Apostles' Creed as an anti-heresy affirmation. While freely granting that it does not represent the words of the apostles, since it did not exist before the middle of the second century, they maintain that it nevertheless represents

[4] In his *History of Christian Thought* (New York: Charles Scribner's Sons, 1932), I, 157.
[5] *Ibid.*, p. 158. I should agree with this statement except that the reference to "Christ Jesus his Son" seems clearly to imply divinity.

the apostolic witness as this was found in the early church.[6]
Whichever of these positions is held, there are significant
facts on which, as far as I know, there is full agreement among
those best informed in early Christian thought. Among
these are: (1) that the Apostles' Creed was not framed by
the first apostles themselves, though credited to their authority, (2) that it omits some very important items of Christian faith, and (3) that it includes the Holy Spirit but tells
us nothing further in this area. This seems to indicate that up
to this time, there had been little of either elaboration of or
argument against the third person of the Trinity.

It was Tertullian who first used the term *una substantia
tres personae*, "one substance, three persons," which has complicated if not bedeviled the understanding of the Trinity
ever since. However, as Tertullian used the term the *personae*
did not mean personal selves, centers of self-consciousness, as
we understand "person" to mean. The basic idea was not
subjective selfhood but objective confrontation. "A person
was a *prosopon*, a 'facing towards' (as the word literally means
in Greek), or a *persona*, a 'sounding through' (as it means
in Latin). . . . *Persona* thus could mean a mask worn by
actors, whereby they confronted the audience with a definite
character and expressed this by his words in a play." [7] This
analogy of the *dramatis personae* as differing roles, each with
a separate function in a related unitary whole, looks in the direction of what was later to be called modalism—three mani-

[6] This position is ably defended by O. Sydney Barr in *From the Apostles' Faith to the Apostles' Creed* (New York: Oxford University Press,
1964).

[7] Cyril C. Richardson, *The Doctrine of the Trinity* (Nashville: Abingdon Press, 1958), p. 63.

festations of one God. However, this formula, once it had been coined and taken over into Greek thought as one *ousia* in three *hypostases,* was destined to dominate Trinitarian thought with various other meanings.

It was not long before modalism was being condemned as heretical. The dominant understanding of the second person of the Trinity, especially in the eastern section of the Church, was the Logos Christology. This in its orthodox form looked upon Christ as the preexistent Son of God, coeternal with God and God's agent in the creation of the world, of one substance with the Father and "begotten" but not created by him. The primary base in Scripture for this view was John 1:1-14 but the Logos Christology was also an attempt to state the nature of the Incarnation in a manner congenial to Greek thought as the faith spread to centers of Hellenic culture.

The idea that Father, Son, and Spirit were three confrontations or manifestations of the one God was considerably at variance with the Logos Christology. Furthermore, modalism was charged with advocating *patripassianism*—the idea that the Father could be thought to suffer. The thought seemed blasphemous to its opponents, though in view of the centrality of the cross in Christian faith the opposition seems strange to us today. Not only was modalism condemned, but with it adoptionism—the belief that God had adopted the human Jesus at his birth or baptism as God's Son and endowed him with supernatural power for his mission of redemption. Both modalism and adoptionism were viewed as forms of monarchianism, stressing the unity (*monarchia*) of the divine nature as against the affirming of personal distinctions within the Triune God. It was the latter that was fast becoming orthodox doctrine.

111

With this brief survey of large issues we must turn to the Nicene controversy. This was precipitated by a clash between Arius and Bishop Alexander of the church at Alexandria, and came to a head at the Council of Nicaea in 325 in a famous contest between Arius and the theologian Athanasius. Both were exponents of a Logos Christology, and while the issue centered in the relation of the *hypostases* of the Trinity to the one *ousia,* the Spirit was not the subject of dispute. The central problem was whether the Son was of the same substance and coeternal with the Father or a subordinate, created being as Arius held him to be. Athanasius won, and a declaration of faith (the original Nicene Creed) was adopted which affirmed in phrase after phrase the full deity and equality of the Son. "We believe in one God, Father Almighty, maker of all things visible and invisible; and in one Lord Jesus Christ the Son of God, begotten of the Father, only-begotten, that is from the substance of the Father, God from God, Light from Light, true God from true God, begotten, not made, of one substance with the Father, through whom all things were made, both the things in heaven and the things on earth. . . ." Yet still there was only the briefest of statements for the third *hypostasis,* "and in the Holy Spirit." This was followed by anathemas for those who believed otherwise, clearly aimed at Arius and his followers.

The first serious attempt to define the Trinity which included attention to the Spirit as well as the Son appears in the writings of three men usually spoken of as the Cappadocian fathers—Basil, his brother Gregory of Nyssa, and Gregory of Nazianzen. Their view was that the three divine *hypostases* each have a separate existence but a common substance, as Peter, James, and John are separate persons but all are men, and that each of the three has a reciprocal relation to the other two. The result of their work tended in the direction of tritheism. However, partly as the result of their influence, when the present Nicene Creed was adopted toward the end of the fourth century, more was said of the Holy Spirit than had previously been affirmed.

This Nicene Creed, almost the same as that which is repeated today in many thousands of services of worship, shows clear traces of the original one with the anathemas omitted, but it is not identical with it. It has often been called the Nicene-Constantinopolitan Creed from the belief that it was adopted at the Council of Constantinople in 381. It is now generally thought to have been based on a fourth-century creed of the Jerusalem church. In any case, it now for the first time in an official statement elaborated the meaning and relationships of the Holy Spirit. While the earlier Nicene Creed had said only, "I believe in the Holy Ghost," this one affirmed, "and in the Holy Ghost, the Lord and Giver of life; who proceedeth from the Father; who with the Father and Son is worshipped and glorified; who spoke through the prophets." It also added statements about the Church, baptism, and the resurrection.

This authentication by reference to the prophets, who spoke relatively little of the Spirit and nothing of the Holy Spirit in the context here indicated, while there is no mention of Paul, the Gospel of John, or the book of Acts where the Holy Spirit is spoken of a great deal, is a curious insertion. It may be due to the high respect in which the prophets were held, or perhaps it is indirectly a witness to the fact that the Spirit speaks to the servants of God at all times and in all places.

The Nicene Creed of the late fourth century was yet to undergo one change to bring it to its present form. The argument over the *filioque,* which was the ostensible ground for the split between the Roman and the Eastern Church in 1054, was already brewing centuries earlier. It had to do with whether the Holy Spirit proceeds from both the Father and the Son, as held in the West, or from the Father only, as maintained by the East. Indirectly, it was the old Arian question, though in a new form, as to the subordination of the Son. Augustine strongly contended for the full equality of the three members of the Trinity, and for the presence of each in every work of the other two. By the end of the sixth century, various groups in the West were altering the Nicene Creed to read "who proceedeth from the Father and the Son," thus annulling any vestige of the subordination of the Son and moving toward the Augustinian view.

So it stands today. Along with the Apostles' Creed, which underwent more gradual changes and did not assume its present form until the eighth century, it has continued to speak both *to* and *for* millions of minds and hearts. It is probably fair to say that relatively few Christians who repeat the words of either of these creeds today in services of worship think very much about their meaning, or have made a serious effort to understand all their affirmations, or are familiar with even these few items of history as to how they took shape. Nevertheless, their great sonorous sentences and the faith to which they point is a permanent possession of the Church, not lightly to be set aside.

4. HOW SHALL WE UNDERSTAND THE TRINITY?

I shall now state what I regard as the simplest and clearest understanding of the Trinity, which is at the same time the most consistent with biblical faith and Christian experience. Not all readers will agree, and others are entitled to hold differing views.

It is a serious misunderstanding to think of Father, Son, and Holy Spirit as three separate deities. This would be polytheism, not monotheism; it would be tritheism, not the Christian trinity. We have noted how Christians, even Christian theologians, have at times been inclined to veer in this direction. This must be staunchly resisted. There is polytheism in primitive religion and in some living non-Christian faiths, such as the triad of Brahama, Siva, and Vishnu in contemporary Hinduism;[8] but it has no legitimate place in Christian faith.

Yet neither is any form of theological unitarianism which denies the unique incarnation of God in Jesus Christ an adequate position. Here we must distinguish between the Unitarian-Universalist Church as a denomination and theological unitarianism. Within the denomination there are various shades of belief, ranging from an atheistic humanism, which had better not be called Christian, to a liberal but genuine emphasis on the uniqueness of the revelation of God in Jesus. This church as a denomination must make up its own mind; what we are concerned with here is the theological unitarianism which in denying the Trinity denies the incarnation. This is as far from the central stream of Christian faith as is a polytheistic tritheism.

[8] Van Dusen, *Spirit, Son and Father*, p. 152, relates an interesting incident which illustrates this Hindu triad.

The best way to steer between these errors, and to be true both to biblical faith and to Christian experience, is to recover the original meaning of *personae* in the *una substantia tres personae* formula. We have noted that it meant not three separate "persons" but three "roles" or manifestations of the one God in the great drama of divine revelation and man's salvation. Numerous analogies besides that of the stage illustrate this relation. There are the historic examples of the upwelling spring of water, the fountain, and the onflowing stream; of the seed or root, the plant, and the flower—of one nature yet not identical. Augustine pointed among other analogies to the triadic relation of memory, understanding, and will within one and the same person.

We cannot erase history. Yet if in place of the Latin *persona* or the Greek *hypostasis* we put the English word *presence*, this comes close to the meaning of both these terms. There is the eternal Presence of God the Creator, Ruler, and Father; the unique, incarnate Presence within history of Jesus Christ the Son; the ongoing, ever-active Presence of the Holy Spirit.

To place the emphasis on the manner in which God reveals himself and brings redemption to man does not remove the mystery of God's love but it does go far toward eliminating the intellectual tangles of the Trinity. One God—the only God—comes to us in three vital, indispensable ways.

God the Father is the loving and almighty maker of heaven and earth, infinite in wisdom, power, goodness, and love. This God has a yearning love for all men as his children and is at work everywhere among men for the increase of righteousness, peace, and joy. Jesus throughout his ministry sought to draw men to the worship and service of God the Father, and it was to this God that he prayed repeatedly and taught his disciples to pray.

God the Son does not mean that Jesus was a second God. Rather, it means that "God was in Christ reconciling the world to himself," and was present in Jesus as the eternal Christ in a way that makes it appropriate to regard him as Lord and Savior. The equality of the Son, on which the early creed makers insisted so rigorously, does not mean a second deity, or even full metaphysical identity with the Father. Otherwise, we should find Jesus praying to and serving himself, a situation not only inherently irrational but contradicted throughout the Gospels. He does say in the Fourth Gospel, "I and the Father are one" (John 10:30), and "He who has seen me has seen the Father" (John 14:9). Yet other passages in close conjunction speak of "the Father who dwells in me" (John 14:10), and refer repeatedly to his going to the Father. In the total context it seems clear that what is being affirmed is Jesus' oneness with the Father in will and purpose and in disclosure of God's love, again in agreement with Paul's affirmation, "God was in Christ." In short, what is being affirmed is the incarnation of God in Christ, not that two gods are somehow one.

This interpretation accords with the deepest notes in the magnificent prologue to John's Gospel. The Word of God, whether this term is applied to the Bible or to Jesus, means God speaking, God disclosing himself. That "the Word became flesh and dwelt among us, full of grace and truth" (John 1:14) is bedrock for Christian faith. So is the sequel, stating the results in immortal words:

117

We have beheld his glory, glory as of the only Son from the Father. . . . And from his fullness have we all received, grace upon grace. For the law was given through Moses; grace and truth came through Jesus Christ. No one has ever seen God; the only Son, who is in the bosom of the Father, he has made him known. (John 1:14-17.)

The New English Bible meaningfully translates the last verse, "God's only Son, he who is nearest to the Father's heart, he has made him known."

With this understanding, it is not difficult to see the place of the Holy Spirit in the Trinity. Again we must guard against thinking of a third God. The Holy Spirit is the same God, the infinite and eternal God, acting in our lives, present with us, here and now. If we follow either Paul's identification of the Holy Spirit with the risen and living Christ or John's record of the promise of the coming Counselor, our thought moves naturally in this direction. It then does not affront either reason, faith, or the biblical witness to think of the Holy Spirit as the Spirit of God that brooded over chaos in creation and was moving in the history of Israel, the eternal divine Spirit that was so clearly manifest in the life, the ministry, the words and work of Jesus, and that did not pass away with his death but is with us forever. Such a conclusion is fully consistent with the affirmation that "God was in Christ reconciling the world to himself," for this process of reconciliation is without end. With the author of the prologue, we who are Christians today can also say, "We have beheld his glory. . . . And from his fullness have we all received, grace upon grace."

In the early days of the Trinitarian controversy, the view

that the three members of the Trinity were modes of disclosure or manifestations of one God was called modalism, or modalistic monarchianism. It was also called Sabellianism from its most famous proponent Sabellius, who contended that the three manifestations appeared successively, one after the other in the sequence of time. Doubtless he was wrong at this point, for the Father and the Holy Spirit, mentioned so little in the Old Testament, were already in existence as one God without beginning or termination. New designations and even new relationships did not bring them into being *de novo*. And what of the preexistent Christ? It affronts our reason to say that the man Jesus lived before Jesus lived; in fact, the incarnation means that he did not. Yet that element of divinity in him which makes him the Christ, the Son of the living God—that divinity which prompts us, like our fathers, to speak of him reverently and gratefully as "the Word made flesh," this did not come into existence with the earthly life of Jesus or disappear with his death. In this sense he is the eternal Christ. As Holy Spirit he is with us still and will be to the end of time, the fulfillment of the promise, "Lo, I am with you always, to the close of the age." [9]

What shall we call this view? While the interpretation that has been presented seems to me too firmly grounded in the Bible and in Christian experience to need a name, modalism will do as well as any if one wishes to affix a label. Heresy? It has many times happened that the heresies of one era become the accepted truths of later generations. We have noted some of the steps by which modalism was condemned

[9] The New English Bible renders this in words somewhat more meaningful to modern ears, "And be assured, I am with you always, to the end of time."

by theologians of the early Church. Yet it contained a truth too life-giving to surrender before charges of heresy. It reappears in Augustine, the greatest theologian of the Western Church, and repeatedly thereafter, more often in the West than in the East. It is widely, though by no means universally, held by theologians today.

Here we shall let the matter rest as far as doctrine is concerned. The continuing presence of the Holy Spirit in the Church, in our own spirits, and in contemporary life must now be our principal concern.

VII

THE HOLY SPIRIT
AND
THE CHURCH

The subject of this chapter is intimately related
to that of the preceding one, and in fact to all that have
preceded it. It is an open question which should be considered
first, the Trinity or the Church. Certainly the Church as an
existing fact, brought into being through the Holy Spirit,
antedates the formulation of trinitarian doctrine and it was
the Church that formulated it. Yet what we shall be mainly
concerned with in this chapter are the various views held
through the centuries as to the relation of the nature of the
Church to the work of the Holy Spirit. This is still an un-
settled question, and because it bears on the matter of denominational divisions and the possibilities of movement
toward Christian unity it is an immensely important one.

1. SOME AGREEMENTS AND DIFFERENCES

It is dangerous to affirm that "all Christians" agree on
anything, for there are all sorts and conditions of men—and
of ideas—among those who "profess and call themselves
Christians." This is the more true since the prevalent secular

climate of the times has invaded churches, and more than a few who think of themselves as Christians have little to tie to in the way of belief unless it be to the ethical imperatives of Jesus. However, among those who still find themselves in the mainstream of Christian belief, who take the Bible seriously, and who find the supreme revelation of the living God in his Son Jesus Christ, there are great agreements. These agreements might be summarized somewhat as follows.

Such a summary would need to begin with an affirmation of belief in God as the Creator and Sustainer of the world and the Judge, Redeemer, and Father of mankind; in Jesus Christ as the Revealer of God and the Savior of men; in the Holy Spirit as God present with us and acting for us to give guidance and strength. To this trinitarian faith would be added the belief that man, though made in the divine image and of infinite worth to God, is nevertheless a sinner unable to save himself. Yet through penitence and acceptance of the forgiving mercy of God, any person can be brought to new life in Christ. This offers hope not only for the earthly scene but for eternal life beyond bodily death through the goodness and power of God.

The Christian hope of salvation stems from the life and ministry, the death, resurrection, and living presence of Jesus Christ. It is epitomized in his central teaching of the kingdom of God. The Christian life centers in faith in God and in love for God and one's fellowmen. It entails not only trust and worship but also the moral obligation of obedience to the will of God in all of life's manifold relationships. The Church as the fellowship of Christ's followers is entrusted with this gospel.

Many issues center in this last statement. Add to it that the

Church is the creation of the Holy Spirit, and the complexities mount. Few Christians would question that the Church is the fellowship of Christ's followers in the sense that this is where Christians meet for worship and other activities. But that the Church not only was originally created but is continually sustained and at times renewed by the Holy Spirit is less self-evident.

What is the Church? Most Christians believe that they ought to join a church, attend it at least occasionally, give it some financial support, and seek its services for baptism, weddings, and funerals. Beyond this, concepts as to the nature of the Church range from the most nebulous idea that the church is a good thing to have in a community to a dogmatic conviction that one's own church is not only the true but the indispensable agent of God for man's salvation. Everybody knows that there are many different kinds of churches, relatively few understand why.

The variety in denominations is linked with the historical circumstances in which they emerged, and sociological as well as theological factors are involved.[1] Nevertheless, deeper than any cultural situation is the nature of the Church itself with its groundwork in Christian faith. If the Church were simply a social institution there would be differences of opinion, as in all other human groups, but these could be tolerantly accepted on the basis of cultural pluralism. This is our official position in American church-state relations, and from this standpoint it is a legitimate one. Yet from the

[1] *The Social Sources of Denominationalism* by H. Richard Niebuhr (New York: Henry Holt and Co., 1929) is still the best presentation of these factors. It has been matched more recently by *The Social Sources of Church Unity* by Robert Lee (Nashville: Abingdon Press, 1960).

standpoint of the Christian's religious loyalties, further issues must be raised. The Church is more than a social institution. It came into being through the Holy Spirit and has a divine mandate to proclaim the gospel of Christ, build up its members in Christ, and serve the world in the spirit of Christ. Its relation to Christ and the Holy Spirit is of crucial importance, for this determines its nature and ultimate authority. Yet this is less agreed upon than any other aspect of Christian faith that was included in the above summary. It is the primary problem of the ecumenical movement.

This is not to imply that Christians, whether lay persons or theologians, agree in every other matter that has been mentioned. There are certainly wide differences of opinion as to just how to think of God, man, Christ, the kingdom, salvation for this life or the next. Yet these differences cut across denominations and follow the lines of conservative, liberal, neo-orthodox, or existentialist thought far more than denominational lines. The issues that separate churches according to polity, or modes of government, forms of worship, the basis of an ordained ministry and the administering and receiving of the sacraments, especially the central sacrament of the Lord's Supper, and the authority of a church over the lives of its members if it can claim such authority, all revolve about the question, "When is a church really the Church?" And this question, in turn, rests back upon the relation of the Church to Christ and the Holy Spirit.

It must now be our task to trace how these differences came about. Very complex movements will of necessity be treated too briefly, but at least the main outlines can be presented.[2]

---

[2] A more extended summary, though from the standpoint of the cleavage in status between clergy and laity rather than the relation of the Holy

2. HOW THE DIFFERENCES CAME ABOUT

a. *In the primitive church.* In the church of the New Testament, often referred to as the primitive or apostolic church, there were differences. When pleas are issued today to return to "the undivided church," the appeal is for something that never existed. John Knox declares with ample evidence to support his statement, "There has never been a time when the church could be truly said to be united." [3] The differences were not denominational, for as yet there were no denominations in the sense of organized bodies of Christians. The differences centered partly in personal tensions, such as prompted Paul to chide the Corinthian church for their quarreling and claiming allegiance to a particular evangelist rather than to Christ (I Cor. 1:11-13). There was also the crucial question, settled in principle at the historic conference recorded in Acts 15 but repeatedly cropping up, of the relation of Gentiles to the Christian fellowship.

However, there are great injunctions to unity within this period, and these are closely connected with the work of the Holy Spirit. New Testament scholars differ in their judgment as to whether Paul wrote the letter to the Ephesians. Yet in this letter stand some of the greatest words about Christian unity that were ever penned. It is the Epistle most directly concerned with the nature and purpose of the Church.

In this letter we find reference after reference to the Spirit as the source and guarantor of Christian unity. Christ "has

Spirit to the Church, is presented in chapters II and III of my *The Church and Its Laity* (Nashville: Abingdon Press, 1962).

[3] *The Early Church and the Coming Great Church* (Nashville: Abingdon Press, 1955), p. 12.

broken down the dividing wall of hostility," and in him we have access in one Spirit to the Father (Eph. 2:14, 18). The Church is the household of God built on the foundation of the apostles and prophets with Jesus Christ as the chief cornerstone, and designed to be a holy temple and dwelling place of God in the Spirit (Eph. 2:19-22). Christ's followers are enjoined to "maintain the unity of the Spirit in the bond of peace," for "there is one body and one Spirit, just as you were called to the one hope that belongs to your call, one Lord, one faith, one baptism" (Eph. 4:3-5). There is, to be sure, a diversity of gifts among Christians but all have their contribution to make "for the equipment of the saints, for the work of ministry, for building up the body of Christ" (Eph. 4:11, 12).[4] It is not by accident that the book of Ephesians is so often today the basis of ecumenical worship and Bible study.

Had these injunctions remained uppermost in the experience of the Church, we should find fewer divisions emerging in the Church throughout the centuries. However, they became overlaid with other factors, including the belief on numerous occasions that the Holy Spirit was leading the people to "come out from among them, and be ye separate." Let us look now at some of these forces.

b. *In Roman Catholicism.* The church of the New Testament and directly thereafter is the common heritage of all Christians. The Roman Catholic Church very much as we now know it—or did know it until the *aggiornamento* of

---

[4] It has been plausibly suggested that since there are no commas in the original Greek this ought to read "for the equipment of the saints for the work of ministry." The New English Bible adopts this rendering with the words, "to equip God's people for work in his service."

Vatican II [5]—was taking shape from the second through the sixth centuries.

We have noted repeatedly the missionary passion of the New Testament church. Indirectly, this was a factor in the crystallization of ecclesiastical authority, for as the church reached out in its witness to new areas each must have its overseer, or bishop. Among these was Rome. While it is unlikely that Peter founded the church at Rome, since he is not mentioned in Paul's letter to the Romans, it is a plausible assumption that he went there later and became its leader. Tradition says both he and Paul were martyred there.

As the soul must function through a body, the churches needed an institutional structure, and in this the bishops became the key figures. And as the primitive church moved from a fluid fellowship of the Spirit to an ecclesiastical body the bishops increased in power. Since they could not be everywhere and the local congregations kept increasing in numbers, the bishops ordained parish priests to represent them. The priests received their authority by the laying on of hands of bishops, who were thought to receive their authority from the apostles, who received their authority from Christ. Thus, the apostolic succession was crucial to the system.

While this structure of authority was developing, the sacramental system was also emerging to provide the channels of salvation, first with the two sacraments of baptism and the Lord's Supper, later with seven. This was linked with the validity of priestly orders in the apostolic succession, and had the effect of placing both temporal and eternal salvation in

[5] Vatican II has not changed the basic structure of the Roman Catholic Church, though it has had important results in such fields as ecumenism, religious liberty, and the relating of the Church to the modern world.

the hands of persons believed to be Christ's authorized representatives.

Provision had also to be made for the purity of the faith. As heresies arose, and as differences of opinion appeared even among the faithful as to the right interpretation of Scripture, somebody must decide the truth. Authority to settle the matter was placed in the bishop as guardian of the faith. But which bishop? As the Church spread over a widening territory unity must be preserved, and episcopal councils seemed at first to be the answer. Yet bishops in council could disagree, and the Church was not ready for the democracy of settling matters by majority vote.

Since the Church must have one head to rule on disputed matters, who could it be but the bishop of Rome? Rome was the "eternal city," the seat of government; it was, furthermore, the See of Peter, to whom, according to Matt. 16:18, 19, Christ himself had given a special commission with promise of authority. The Church now had a Pope, successor of Peter and vice-gerent of Christ. While the dogma of papal infallibility in faith and morals was not officially promulgated until 1870, the Pope had long before that time been regarded in this light.

What of the Holy Spirit in this process? The Roman Church has never denied the existence or the agency of the Holy Spirit, and it is staunchly trinitarian in its faith. Nevertheless, from the early centuries to the present it has channeled the work of the Holy Spirit through the Church. This has had the effect, however unintentional, of subordinating the authority of the Holy Spirit.

A key to this subordination is found in the fact that there are two passages in the New Testament to appeal to for the coming into existence of the Church, in Matthew 16 and Acts 2. The Roman Church centers its scriptural authority in the first of these, and makes much of Christ's word to Peter. Luther also made much of Matthew 16, but held that the founding of the Church centered in Peter's word, "You are the Christ, the Son of the living God." This has been the usual Protestant position but with the addition of a strong emphasis on the coming of the Holy Spirit at Pentecost. Pentecost is not denied in the Catholic structure, but it has never been greatly accented. What is put foremost is the "instituting" of the Church by Christ's words to Peter rather than the transforming experience of fellowship in Christ through the gift and power of the Holy Spirit. The difference has been aptly put in these words:

Perhaps the fundamental difference between Roman Catholic and Protestant on the beginning of the Church is just here; for the Roman Catholic it is instituted, for the Protestant it is created. For the one it begins with an official word of authority, for the other it comes as the act of the living Spirit of God.[6]

The Holy Spirit in Roman Catholic thought thus occupies a somewhat ambiguous position, ostensibly directing the Church but being interpreted and channeled through the Church. From Pope through the Councils to the humblest of the faithful, the guidance and strengthening of the Spirit is acknowledged. Yet the Spirit guarantees the infallibility of the *magisterium,* or rulership, and this *magisterium* has the final say. The gifts of the Holy Spirit are imparted through

[6] Hugh Vernon White in a paper on "The Role of the Holy Spirit in the Church's Quest for God" presented before the Pacific Coast Theological Group.

the sacraments; yet the sacraments are valid only through the proper authorization within the apostolic succession. In matters of dogma or true belief, which in the Roman Catholic system is derived both from Scripture and tradition, the Church led by the Spirit decides what is true. The Church in this context means the Pope, with or without the "collegiality" of the bishops.[7] Then the faithful are to accept it.

This interplay, in which the Holy Spirit appears to direct but in effect is directed by the Church, becomes clearer in terms of the distinction drawn between the "higher" and "inferior" members of the Church. Pope Pius XII in his encyclical *Mystici corporis* issued in 1943 stresses the fact that the Holy Spirit "is personally present and divinely active in all the members," yet he adds that "in the inferior members he acts also through the higher members."[8] Since the inferior members are the laity and the higher the clergy with the *magisterium* of the clergy culminating in the Pope, the ecclesiastical hierarchy becomes the normative channel through which the Spirit speaks to the people.

It was this kind of canalizing that called forth the Protestant Reformation. That it could not constrict the Spirit to a single course is evidenced not only in the devotional piety that never died out, but still more in the remarkable movements of the twelfth through the fourteenth centuries that produced Saint Francis, the Waldensians, the Friends of God, the Brethren of the Common Life, and such mystical

[7] The authority of the college of bishops cannot be exercised without the consent of the Pope, who is its head, while he can act apart from the bishops.

[8] Quoted by George S. Hendry in *The Holy Spirit in Christian Theology*, p. 59.

writers as Meister Eckhart, John Tauler, Thomas à Kempis [9] and the unknown author of the *Theologia Germanica*. The Spirit "bloweth where it listeth" even under ecclesiastical control, and this was the case in these movements. While it is too soon to judge final results, this appears also to be true in various aspects of the new freedom that has emerged from the Second Vatican Council, though the main core of the *magisterium* has been retained.

c. *In Eastern Orthodoxy*. As was noted in the preceding chapter, the first great schism in the Church took place in 1054, ostensibly over the *filioque* which the Western Church had added to the Nicene Creed to say that the Holy Spirit proceeds from the Father "and the Son" instead of the Father only. Actually, however, the split was due much more to social and political rivalries and differences in theological temperament than to this particular issue over the Holy Spirit.

Once separated, the two churches took different, though not wholly different, courses. The apostolic succession with its validation of the authority of bishops and priests, and hence of the sacraments, was retained. So, too, was the veneration of the saints and especially of the Blessed Virgin. Without a Pope and with various regional groups emerging which followed ethnic and national rather than theological lines, Eastern Orthodoxy became a loose affiliation of independent churches, each with its own patriarch.[10] They are united by

[9] While the original form of the *Imitation of Christ* was probably written by Gerhard Groote, a leading figure in the religious fellowship who called themselves Brothers of the Common Life, Thomas à Kempis as editor and co-author still merits the renown that history has given him.

[10] Officially but with little direct jurisdiction over the other regional "autocephalous" branches of Eastern Orthodoxy, the patriarch of Constan-

a common liturgy, though in the vernacular of each country, and still more by a common conviction of a source of authority which makes Orthodoxy the one true church.

This source of authority, in Orthodox thinking, lies in the pronouncements of the seven ecumenical councils of the early centuries of the Church. These have special authority on the ground that the Church was then undivided. The Holy Spirit has spoken there to authenticate these decisions; there is no need for him to speak again in matters of faith. Orthodoxy alone is custodian of this divinely given truth, untarnished by human error.

An example of what has been called this "sweet intransigeance" is seen in the words of the Most Reverend Athenagoras, Archbishop of Thyateira, as he addressed the World Conference on Faith and Order at Lund in 1952:

> The Greek Orthodox Church knows and proclaims that She is not dealing with human teaching and human precepts but with divine ones and no one has the right to confuse these with individual opinion about them. She is the whole and only Church, the Body of Christ, the only mandatory agent of the Apostles. So She only can define the Faith. . . . And we are sure that this is a proof of her uniqueness. . . .
>
> We do not come to criticize other Churches but to help them, to illuminate their mind in a brotherly manner by informing them about the teaching of the One Holy, Catholic and Apostolic Church which is the Greek Orthodox Church, unchanged since the apostolic era.[11]

---

tinople is the head of the Orthodox churches. This is what made the brotherly meeting between him and Pope Paul VI in January, 1964 of such historic importance.

[11] Quoted by Hugh Vernon White, "The Role of the Holy Spirit in the Church's Quest for God."

Is this a case of "absolutizing the relative"? So it would seem to those outside of this communion. Yet other churches do it too, though usually with less direct affirmation. A perennial temptation besets both individuals and churches to claim the Holy Spirit's sanction for what human minds earnestly believe.

Before judging too harshly these structures of faith and order which have been relatively unchanged since their beginnings, as Protestants are prone to do, two considerations need to be taken into account. The first is the tension which always exists between freedom and order, the second is the interplay of conserving and forward-looking forces.

The Holy Spirit is not restricted to one or the other of these movements. It is more obviously the channel of freedom than of order in the life of the Christian believer—a freedom which emancipates the inner life of the individual even when many are associated in a fellowship. This happened at Pentecost and is echoed throughout Paul's letters. Nevertheless, "For freedom Christ has set us free" is not Paul's only word. The main emphasis of First Corinthians 14 is the superiority of prophecy, which we should probably call preaching, instruction, and understanding of the gospel, to speaking in tongues, though the last is not forbidden. The chapter ends with the definitive words of counsel, "All things should be done decently and in order" (vs. 40). It was the attempt to keep the Church within proper order that led the Roman Church in the formative centuries to resist the Montanists and the Donatists,[12] and has actuated both the Roman and

[12] The Montanists were a group emerging toward the end of the second century who, somewhat like the Pentecostals of today, believed that the Holy Spirit was prompting them to ecstatic utterance, ascetic standards

Eastern churches to resist any radical departure from accepted ways.

The Church has a divine mandate to carry its witness forward, sustained by the presence of Christ "to the end of the age." Yet it is also obligated to look backward to its sources as these are found in the Bible. Furthermore, the Scripture must be interpreted and its message apprehended. Thus far, there is little disagreement among Christians. But how is this to be done? The Church as the Mystical Body of Christ, so runs the argument, must through its Pope and bishops, or through its historic councils, declare the meaning and message of Scripture and tradition. The Holy Spirit speaks through the Church in its affirmations from the past but into the life of today.

Such a conviction allows for little deviation in what is affirmed, or acknowledgment of error in regard to sacred mysteries. Yet it does not rule out human shortcomings or beget more self-righteousness than is found elsewhere. In assemblies of the World Council of Churches Protestants have often been disturbed by assertions of the Orthodox members that the Church cannot sin. This would be better understood if such a statement as this by a distinguished Orthodox theologian were taken into account:

The principle of the "Church reformed and always to be reformed" can and must be applied, in Orthodoxy, to those

---

of morality, and an emphasis on the imminent Second Coming of Christ. Since they placed the authority of the Spirit above that of the Church, they were suppressed. The Donatists insisted, in opposition to Augustine, that the validity of the sacraments did not rest solely on the authority of the Church but was conditional on the personal character of the bishop or priest who performed the rite.

elements which are only human—and they are many in the historical Church—but that which *God gives to us,* the divine presence of his fulness in us and among us, in the sacraments and in the Truth preserved by the Holy Spirit in the Church, is above and beyond "reformation." [13]

d. *Reformation Protestantism.* Contemporary Protestantism is of four main types, proliferating into a great many denominations. First, there is what is often called "classical Protestantism," the types represented by the Lutheran and Calvinist traditions. There is Anglicanism, which ranges all the way from an Anglo-Catholicism with strongly Catholic leanings to a "low church," which is nearly the "free church," position. There is that large group of Methodists, Baptists, Congregationalists (now United Church of Christ), Disciples, and other smaller denominations which for lack of a better term are often referred to as the free churches, although the other meaning of this term in regard to church-state relations makes this a very ambiguous designation. And there is that still freer group in which extremes meet—the Holiness and Pentecostal sects on the one hand and the Unitarian-Universalist fellowship on the other, with the Society of Friends sharing in some characteristics of each without belonging to either.

Again we must limit attention to what these groups think about the nature of the Church and its relation to the Holy Spirit. Let us begin with Luther and Calvin, progenitors of

[13] John Meyendorff in "The Significance of the Reformation in the History of Christendom," *The Ecumenical Review,* XVI (1964), 173.

Lutheranism and, historically, of the Presbyterian and Reformed churches of today.[14]

It is well known that the Protestant Reformation came about as a result of abuses in the Roman church, particularly in regard to the sale of indulgences, and also from social and political conditions which called for protest against domination by the Church. Furthermore, the Reformers believed that the Scriptures had been violated. Yet this was not all.

It was still held as a theoretical belief that the Holy Spirit acted behind and through the agents and acts of the Church, and it was invoked as the source of the dogma and authority of the hierarchy, but the lower agents occupied the whole field of men's vision and interest, so that the doctrine of the Spirit had no longer any ground in religious experience.[15]

In connection with this loss of a living and present sense of the Holy Spirit's work, Hendry also points out that the apostles, who had been commissioned to *witness* to Christ, had come to be regarded as Christ's *successors*. This made the Church through the apostolic succession the voice of Christ on earth, thus assuming the role of the Spirit in reversal of the promise given by Christ as recorded in the Gospel of John.[16]

Into this situation came Martin Luther and, a little later, John Calvin. Both men profoundly believed that in their

[14] Contemporary Presbyterian and Reformed churches, in many respects affiliated with the "free church" group, seem less closely linked theologically with Calvin than Lutheranism with Luther.

[15] T. Rees, *The Holy Spirit in Thought and Experience* (New York: Charles Scribner's Sons, 1915), p. 174.

[16] George S. Hendry, *The Holy Spirit in Christian Theology*, pp. 63-67.

break with the Roman church they were actuated by the Holy Spirit, and they spoke in defense of "the liberty of the Christian man," as Luther phrased it, against the hierarchical control of the Roman church. Yet for them, as for their predecessors, order must also be maintained. Both men grounded their authority in the Scriptures, and the Scriptures were not to be read with a slavish literalism but interpreted through the *testimonium Spiritus Sancti.* In Calvin this internal authority of the Holy Spirit was accompanied by rigorous external authority for the preservation of Christian morality and the Protestant faith within the Genevan theocracy.

Luther left no treatise on the relation of the Holy Spirit to the Church, and his views on the Spirit must be gleaned largely from references in other connections. Yet these are discernible at three points of great centrality to his thought; the doctrines of justification by faith, the Word, and the sacraments.

It has been said of him, "Luther was essentially a man of one idea; and that idea was Justification by Faith." [17] Canon Dewar, an Anglican who makes this judgment, says also that this "one-track-mindedness" impaired him as a biblical commentator and obscured his insight into the biblical doctrine of the Holy Spirit. While I do not share all of this author's deductions the statement has much truth.

Luther's dominant emphasis on justification by faith stresses the divine initiative, the individual's personal access to God and his transformation of life through faith in Christ, which remains an essential Protestant note. Yet it tends to make the experience of Paul and of Luther himself normative for all

[17] Lindsay Dewar, *The Holy Spirit and Modern Thought,* p. 125.

Christians. The manifold means of grace through which the Holy Spirit works are circumscribed by a too exclusive emphasis on the justification of the sinner through faith alone.

To Luther as to most Protestants today, "the Word" means either Christ as God's self-disclosure, magnificently stated in John 1:1-18, or the gospel of Christ to be preached in his Church, or the Holy Bible. Christ imparts faith to Christian believers, and this Word is to be proclaimed from Christian pulpits. However, in matters of truth the Bible is the final authority.

This emphasis gave rise to the *sola scriptura* of the Reformation in opposition to the Church as the determiner of dogma. Luther was by no means the literalist that many later Protestants became. In addition to his well-known repudiation of the letter of James as "an epistle of straw" because of its emphasis on works, he rejected the traditional belief that Solomon was the author of Ecclesiastes and he rather wished to see the book of Esther eliminated from the Old Testament because of its over-nationalistic Jewish sentiment. The statements in Hebrews 6:4-6 and in 10:26-31 that there is no possibility of repentance or forgiveness for the backslider seemed to him incompatible with the writings of Paul and with the Christian gospel. Nevertheless, he believed the Bible to be the inspired word of God, not the *record* of the Word but the Word itself through which God speaks.

How is the Bible to be interpreted so that the unity of the Church may be preserved? Through the Holy Spirit. However, Luther's answer lacks precision and is not elaborated. He insists that the inward witness of the Spirit interprets the Word "through the gospel" which "effects regeneration and renewal, whose first and essential element is faith." [18] Thus, in substance, true interpretation and hence true belief hinge on justification by faith.

The sacraments were not to Luther the exclusive means of grace that they were to his predecessors. Together with preaching they are a medium for the proclamation of the Word. Reduced to the two "dominical" sacraments for which authorization is found in the Bible, they are channels through which the Holy Spirit acts to impart grace to the believer. The sacrament of the Lord's Supper gets its authenticity from the Real Presence of Christ, "in, with, and under" the material elements of bread and wine. Yet even unworthy communicants may receive Christ's body, for it is God's grace and not man's merit that is at the heart of the matter.

John Calvin, less mystical and more legalistic by temperament and training, went considerably further than Luther in stressing the inerrancy of the Bible as the inspired Word. While he was not a fundamentalist in the usual modern sense, he gave to his successors an impulse in this direction of which we have not yet seen the last. It is no accident that in the twentieth century the fundamentalist-modernist controversy has rent the Presbyterian church more than any other major denomination.

The most famous of all his words on the subject are these:

There is this difference between the Apostles and their successors, they were sure and authentic amanuenses of the Holy Spirit; and, therefore, their writings are to be regarded as the

[18] Reinhold Seeberg, *Textbook of the History of Doctrines* (Grand Rapids, Mich.: Baker Book House), II, 256.

oracles of God, whereas others have no other office than to teach what is sealed and delivered in the Holy Scriptures.[19]

However, it would be unfair to Calvin's memory to suggest that he was indifferent to the problems left by these "sure and authentic amanuenses." He was well aware that the Bible requires interpretation. Here again it is the Holy Spirit, enlightening the eyes of the elect, that enables the believer to discern the truth. Man's rational faculties, useful in many spheres, are insufficient at this point. "The Word of God is like the sun which shines upon all, but is of no use to the blind; hence the Word cannot penetrate the mind unless the Spirit, that internal teacher, by His enlightening power make an entrance for it." [20] The believer's assurance of "a divine energy living and breathing in it" [21] authenticates the Scripture, and this assurance the Holy Spirit gives.

Calvin followed Luther in conceiving the Church as a fellowship of Christian believers, individually saved by grace through faith and not by works. Yet he was considerably more rigorous than Luther in insisting that the elected and redeemed Christian is saved *to* good works and a fitting life of moral purity. This is reflected in the disciplines imposed to make Geneva a moral city and in his care to guard the Lord's table from those he deemed unfit to approach it.

On the positive side, Calvin grounded the Church on biblical theology and laid strong emphasis on the internal testimony of the Holy Spirit. He believed he was affirming an infallible and objective authority for Christian faith and

---

[19] *The Institutes of the Christian Religion*, Book IV, viii, 9.
[20] *Ibid.*, Book III, ii, 34.
[21] *Ibid.*, Book I, vii, 5.

morals, not subject to the human frailty which had produced the abuses against which the Reformation was protesting. It is one of the ironies of history that he opened the door to a biblical literalism that was to become a formidable foe to the very ends he was seeking to achieve.

e. *Later Protestantism.* We shall conclude the chapter with a brief look at other forms of ecclesiology in relation to the Holy Spirit, though with no more than a hint of the direction in which the main types move.

The *Anglican* Church is also a product of the Reformation, though not in its mainstream and hence too often by-passed in discussion of the roots of Protestantism. It has both Catholic and Protestant elements—a factor which makes it a *via media* and hence a very significant contributor to the modern ecumenical movement.

In relation to the Holy Spirit, its major notes appear to be these: emphasis on the corporate rather than the individual action of the Spirit; the Spirit of order, mediated through the historic episcopate; and the lifting up of the sacraments as the Spirit's indispensable if not sole channel for the imparting of grace. All three notes are closely related.

In the discussion by Canon Dewar to which reference has been made, the basic error he finds in both Luther and Calvin is that they put the emphasis on the justification and regeneration of the individual rather than on the corporate empowering and guidance of the Church through the Holy Spirit.[22] This is typical of the Catholic rather than the Protestant principle within Anglicanism. Other exponents of the Anglican, or in America the Protestant Episcopal, position

---

[22] *The Holy Spirit and Modern Thought,* pp. 125-48.

retain the historic episcopate, not because they believe it is "historic" in the sense that it can be validated by the New Testament, but because it seems to them a fitting channel by which the order, dignity, and continuity of the Church is preserved. The sacraments, duly administered within this order, become the primary vehicle of the Holy Spirit. Much emphasis is laid on the imparting of the Holy Spirit through baptism as this marks incorporation into Christ's body, the Church, and in keeping with this principle only baptized Christians are invited to receive the sacrament of Holy Communion. The churches vary as to whether *all* baptized Christians are to be thus invited, or only those who have received this rite within the Anglican structure of faith and order. The possibility of intercommunion remains one of the most knotty problems of the ecumenical movement.

The *Methodist* Church stands midway between the classical Reformation and the Anglican positions, drawing from both sources without duplicating either. It has an emphasis on the Holy Spirit which may well constitute a distinctive contribution to the ecumenical movement of today.

In the writings of John Wesley there is no extensive spelling out of ecclesiology or of the doctrinal aspects of the third person of the Trinity. The reason is obvious, for his prime concern was with what he called Scriptural holiness—the bringing of men to new life in Christ, their growth in grace and upbuilding in the Christian life. Competent theologian though he was, Christian experience was to Wesley what mattered. Yet the Holy Spirit was central to this experience.

Justification by faith alone was as essential a note to Wesley as to the Reformers. No man is saved by his own merit or good works, only by the grace of God as this comes to the penitent sinner through Christ. In summarizing "the principles of a Methodist" he put it thus, "Our main doctrines, which include all the rest, are three—that of repentance, of faith, and of holiness. The first of these we account, as it were, the porch of religion; the next, the door; the third, religion itself." [23]

However, Wesley broke completely with the Reformers' doctrine of election. Universal salvation is available through Christ to any who will receive it in penitence by faith. The witness of the Spirit gives assurance of one's forgiveness and reconciliation to God. From this point forward, holiness of heart and life is both God's gift and the Christian's goal. Regeneration occurs at the moment of justification by faith when the penitent sinner accepts Christ as his Savior; sanctification is the ongoing process of being made perfect in love and hence in the fruits of faith.

To Wesley the Holy Spirit is present in God's prevenient grace before as well as after conversion, and is always present to serve the needs of men. Yet it is in the witness of the Spirit, or Christian assurance, and in the quest for Christian perfection, or holiness of living, that the Spirit's work is most clearly manifest. These notes though in modified forms continue in Methodism to the present, while Wesley's more questionable emphasis on the possibility of entire sanctification has for the most part been repudiated.

Though Wesley remained within the Church of England all his life, at two points his emphasis differed notably. The immediate effect of his preaching of the new birth to be fol-

[23] Quoted by S. Paul Schilling in *Methodism and Society in Theological Perspective* (Nashville: Abingdon Press, 1960), p. 45.

lowed by the witness of the Spirit to its reality called forth charges of fanaticism and "enthusiasm," hence opposition. A second effect, less evident at first but more permanent, relates to the sacraments. These were to Wesley the symbol and seal of the new birth but not its instruments. Baptism is the sign, regeneration is the thing signified; water is not the same as the Spirit, and they are not always found together. To the present the ritual for the Lord's Supper in Methodism follows the Anglican form but with an open invitation to any who feel they can meet the spiritual requirements.

The *free churches* constitute the rest of Protestantism, though both the Presbyterians and Methodists whose roots we have traced are usually considered among this group. As early sects with a distinctive emphasis, the Anabaptists, Moravians, and Mennonites had emerged before Luther and Calvin finished their work. In various forms they have continued to proliferate to the present. The major existing free church denominations in addition to those named, if stated in the order of their appearance, are the Baptists, Congregationalists (now the United Church of Christ), Quakers or Society of Friends, Church of the Brethren, Evangelical-United Brethren, and Disciples of Christ. There are also various subdivisions of these groups and many small Holiness or Pentecostal sects. The Unitarians, following a quite different line, were in existence by the sixteenth century but not fully organized until the nineteenth.

This total group is sometimes referred to as "radical Protestantism." This is hardly an accurate term, for while they began as sects, or minority movements with a particular emphasis, most of them dropped their "radicalism" as they increased in numbers and in general recognition as established churches. The Anabaptists, as offensive to Luther as was the Roman Church, were persecuted out of existence. The Mennonites, Quakers, and Church of the Brethren remain to the present the historic peace churches, committed to pacifism in regard to war and to service to human need across international lines. Small Moravian groups still exist. The Holiness sects, in addition to being adventist in regard to the second coming of Christ, stress the saving of souls and emotional fervor in what they regard as an outpouring of the Holy Spirit. The Unitarians decry this approach in favor of a reasoned faith, liberal theology, and social action. The other groups mentioned above have moved from the "sect" to the "church" stage of development, if we adopt the now classic distinction introduced by Ernst Troeltsch. As a result, in spite of differences in polity and practice, their points of agreement outweigh the differences.

Is there a common element in these groups? Certainly, the free churches contain strange bedfellows! Among them are literalists and liberals; some are committed to social action while others decry it; some have a strong doctrine of the Church and others virtually none. However, a common feature emerges in an emphasis on the immediacy of the Christian's access to God through the Holy Spirit. Neither Bible nor Church is central. What matters most is to be a follower of Jesus Christ and to listen and obey as the Holy Spirit speaks to Christ's followers today.

This is not to say that in these churches either Bible or Church is unimportant. Yet they are not all-important. Henry Van Dusen has admirably summarized the distinctive position of this varied group in reference to the Holy Spirit under two heads:

145

1. That the leading of the Holy Spirit is not confined to the confirmation of the words of Scripture, but guides into "new truth" which God desires to reveal to His children in the special and novel circumstances of their contemporary life.
2. That the operation of the Holy Spirit is not limited to the channels and officials of the institutional Church, but comes directly to expectant and contrite spirits in our time as it has through all the ages.[24]

Throughout this survey we have found every type of Christian church claiming the authority of the Holy Spirit. Can all be right? That there are grounds of unity at a common center is implicit in the fact that all regard themselves as Christian churches, and most of them would affirm their faith in God as Father, Son, and Holy Spirit. Yet the temptation to claim the Holy Spirit's sanction for deep-seated conviction forever haunts the human spirit.

In the next chapter, we must face this problem head on. When does God speak? When am *I* speaking to *me*? That is the question.

[24] *Spirit, Son and Father*, pp. 136-37.

VIII

HUMAN SPIRIT
AND
HOLY SPIRIT

Before moving to an attempt to answer the crucial question posed at the end of the previous chapter it is necessary to do something which has, for the most part, been intentionally bypassed to this point. This is the question of what the human spirit meant to the biblical writers and what it means, with some variants and additions, to the man of today.

Unless there is some affinity between man and God, or at the least some relationship which makes communion and communication possible, there is not much use of speaking about the guidance and strengthening of man by the Holy Spirit. Nor, for that matter, does prayer mean anything more than talking to oneself. Prayer has obvious subjective benefits, but these benefits disappear when its objectivity is denied. This question, then, is far more than an academic one; it lies at the very base of religious experience.

We shall look first at the biblical understanding of man's nature and, in particular, what it appears to mean by the human spirit. This will call for some evaluation of the extent

147

to which the biblical view accords with today's knowledge. After that, we shall be ready to consider by what criteria we may distinguish the voice of the Spirit from the clamor of our own desires and the impulses that keep welling up from the human subconscious mind.

1. THE BIBLICAL VIEW OF MAN

The term "spirit" is used in the Bible in so many contexts that it will be helpful first to take a general look at the biblical understanding of man. In spite of some inconsistencies it contains great agreements which have set the tone of Christian thinking through many centuries.

First, our total existence, both body and soul, is derived from God. He alone is the Creator in any ultimate sense; we are his creatures though with a delegated creativity better understood as responsible stewardship. The early "J" story of man's creation in Genesis 2:7 and the later "P" account in Genesis 1:27, 28 state positively what is implied thereafter, though there is little subsequent reference to the divine image in man. The fact that these stories reflect intuitive judgments couched in mythological language rather than scientific descriptions of human origins by no means detracts from their great significance.

Second, man is God's supreme creation, not to be identified with the animals and inanimate things that God has made. To be sure, man is not wholly different. The word *nephesh*, which means "life" or "soul" or "living being" applies to the animals as well. In fairness to the Hebrew text, the translators of the Revised Standard Version rendered Genesis 2:7 as "man became a living being," for the "living soul" of the

King James Version suggests too wide a separation. The author of Ecclesiastes, more Greek than Hebrew in his thinking, affirms the same fate for the sons of men and for the beasts, "All go to one place; all are from the dust, and all turn to dust again" (3:20). Yet the primary overtones of the biblical message are of man's difference from and superiority over the rest of the created world. This is affirmed explicitly in such passages as Psalms 8:5, 6 and Matthew 6:25-30; 10:31; 12:12; it is implied throughout in the fact that it is man's sinning that displeases God and man's salvation toward which God's mercy and love are directed.

Third, man stands in the dual relationship of being made in the image of God, yet nevertheless an inveterate sinner. This lies at the root of what Blaise Pascal called "the grandeur and the misery of man." One may stress either the dignity of man or his persistent sinfulness and be on safe ground; what it is not possible to do without distortion is to center attention on either of these aspects of man's ambivalent nature in disregard of the other.

There is no unanimity among theologians as to what is meant by the *imago dei,* or the divine image in man. It has often been identified with man's rational faculties, whereby man alone shows marked supremacy over the rest of the animate world by his intellectual quests, his problem-solving, his system-making. This view has been especially prominent in Roman Catholic thought because of the influence of Aristotle on St. Thomas Aquinas in his compilation of the *Summa Theologica,* still regarded as a basic formulation of Catholic doctrine. However, it may be doubted that man's reason is the most distinctive note in the image of God. This concept is more largely a heritage from Greek than from biblical thought. Furthermore, if one wishes to try to define what is characteristically human in contrast with the subhuman animal, the borderline between human and animal intelligence defies sharp separation.

A more acceptable criterion of the distinctive note in the *imago dei* is man's moral consciousness. Man alone has that freedom of will and decision which enables him to be a morally responsible being, able to obey or to sin against his Creator. While the metaphysical and psychological aspects of man's moral freedom are not spelled out in the Bible, as one could hardly expect them to be, the Bible centers not only in the goodness of God but in his demand for goodness in man through faithful obedience. Goodness, whether viewed as righteousness or in warmer terms as love, mercy, and forgiveness, is meaningless without moral freedom. It lies at the heart of what is meant by a personal God and by personality in man.

Man's freedom and hence his responsibility are implied throughout the Bible; yet no claim is made that this freedom is absolute. On the contrary, man encounters obstacles at every turn. There are barriers to the freedom of action in one's own nature, as Paul vividly sets forth in Romans 7. Limits are set by the forces of nature, by the acts of other persons, by God himself. Nevertheless, man is responsible. The Bible knows nothing of the deterministic view, current in much present-day psychology and sociology, which denies the reality of sin or finds an alibi for sin in mitigating factors beyond one's control.

In close connection with man's moral freedom as basic to the divine image is man's impulse to worship and capacity for worship. This the human creature has in distinction from all other beings God has made. The Bible does not elaborate this point, but it does reflect throughout man's need to worship and adore, as well as to trust and obey, the Most High God. Idolatry appears wherever such worship is directed to anything less than the Lord of all the earth.

While the note of moral responsibility through a God-given freedom and man's need to worship the Unseen are basic to the *imago dei*, these ramify into the totality of human life. The divine image in man is better defined by modes of approach than by specific categories. Two which are essential may be thus summarized. (1) Instead of taking the animal world as a base line, as is often done in the attempt to get at what is most distinctively human, it is more accurate to take into account those qualities in which humans do show some kinship, however faint and distorted by sin, to the attributes of God. While "no man hath seen God at any time," the Bible gives us a clear enough picture which comes to focus in Jesus. Without undue presumption, the Christian knows that his God is a God of love, mercy, forgiveness, responsible goodness in an inclusive sense, and at the same time of power, wisdom, continuous creativity, and as evidenced by his world, the love of beauty. (2) The divine image means that man is made for fellowship with God as well as for the worship of God. There is that within man which cannot be at ease until he finds his center and point of both rest and action in God. St. Augustine expressed this perfectly when he wrote, "Thou awakest us to delight in Thy praise; for Thou madest us for Thyself, and our heart is restless, until it repose in Thee." [1]

[1] *Confessions*, I, 1.

151

From both of these angles, the relation of the image of God in man to the Holy Spirit is of central importance. It is man's kinship with God that gives him an awareness of the call to moral obedience, the possibility of sin when this call is thwarted by self-love and self-righteousness, the assurance of forgiveness and strengthening for the new life which God's love offers to the penitent. Furthermore, the divine image is basic to the communion of the human spirit with the Spirit of God, whether in private prayer or corporate worship, and hence to the sources of religious aspiration and devotion. Without it, there could be no sense of divine guidance or the undergirding of divine support.

In the fourth place, to note another aspect of the biblical understanding of the nature of man, the person is one being. That is to say, the biblical writers did not ordinarily think of man as a duality of a physical body and a separable soul temporarily residing in it. The latter view, still very common in popular thought, is more Platonic than biblical, though it is retained more from the pull of tradition and a wistfulness to think of the souls of one's loved ones as living on without the body than from any general knowledge of Plato. It must be said immediately that one may accept the somatic unity of body and spirit, and still believe in eternal life through the goodness and power of God. Yet to the biblical mind, there was no sharp line between the psychic and the physical which would permit the body to die and the soul to live on in dissociation from it. This accounts for the fact that resurrection rather than immortality is the usual term for God's conquest of death and the imparting of eternal life.[2]

[2] If the reader wishes to pursue further my views on this matter, he may

152

Nevertheless, it is not to be assumed that no distinction was drawn between the body and the soul of the individual person. In the Old Testament there are some intimations of a separable soul which upon death makes its abode in Sheol. In Isaiah 14:9-20 is a vivid picture of the disillusioning welcome given to the proud and haughty upon their arrival in Sheol. In still earlier writing there are reflections of the ghost-soul common in primitive religions, and Saul's request to the witch (or medium) of Endor to call up Samuel for counsel (I Sam. 28:3-19) may be an example of this.

In the main, however, the biblical writers regarded the body-soul relation as a unity within which there are not separate parts though there are differing bodily and "soulish" functions. Jesus is reported as saying, "And do not fear those who kill the body but cannot kill the soul; rather fear him who can destroy both soul and body in hell" (Matt. 10:28; cf. also Luke 12:4). Paul urged the Corinthians not to sin against their bodies, for "your body is a temple of the Holy Spirit within you" (I Cor. 6:18-20). He also made it clear that the body must be kept in subjection to higher goals and purposes (I Cor. 9:27). Even in regard to the final destiny of the individual he did not hesitate to use the term "immortality" in First Corinthians 15, and his understanding of the nature of the future life appears to have been of a spiritual body continuous but not identical with the physical body we know on earth.

The word "flesh" is an ambiguous term which appears in the Bible with a variety of meanings. It may connote simply the body. But it also can mean the human person in his

find them in *Our Christian Hope* (Nashville: Abingdon Press, 1964), chap. VI.

totality. Or it can mean, especially in Paul's usage, the natural man unredeemed by the Spirit of God. The meaning must be judged by the context, and it is a mistake either to equate the flesh with the body in all passages or to regard the body as necessarily the source of evil. In the basic affirmation of the incarnation in John's Gospel, "The Word became flesh and dwelt among us," it means that the Son of God became a human being. In the Old Testament, "flesh" usually means the body or some part of it, but in numerous references to "all flesh" the context clearly indicates "all persons."

It is in Paul's writing that the contrast between flesh and spirit is most prominent. Significantly, this contrast is interwoven with references to the Spirit of God. Yet Paul does not always use the contrasting terms in the same sense, and we shall misunderstand him if we do not recognize this fact. In Galatians 3:1-5 the "works of the law" are contrasted with "hearing with faith," the flesh being the source of the former and the Spirit the latter. "Did you receive the Spirit by works of the law, or by hearing with faith? Are you so foolish? Having begun with the Spirit, are you now ending with the flesh?" (Gal. 3:2-3). This would seem to equate the flesh with the natural man who can achieve some measure of goodness, inadequate though it be, by obedience to the law.

Two chapters further along in the letter to the Galatians Paul draws the sharpest possible contrast between the works of the flesh which are unequivocally evil and the fruit of the Spirit which is love, joy, peace, patience, kindness, goodness, faithfulness, gentleness, self-control (Gal. 5:22-23). However, a brief examination of the fifteen works of the flesh which are enumerated and condemned as contrary to the desires of the

Spirit will indicate that they by no means all proceed from bodily impulses. Paul was not interested in making psychological distinctions. What was all-important to him was that the Spirit of God should rule and transform the total life of those who belong to Christ.

2. WHAT IS THE HUMAN SPIRIT?

The biblical view of man, as it has been summarized in the preceding section, gives groundwork for seeing the relation of the human spirit to the Holy Spirit. Man is God's supreme creation, with a duty and a destiny beyond that of any other creature, the object of God's special love and saving concern. He is made in the spiritual image of God, and this carries with it both great responsibilities and great grounds of hope. Body and soul together, he comes from God, his destiny is in God's hands, and through Christ he is called by God to manifest in his living the fruit of the Spirit.

We must now become more specific, and ask two important questions. When the biblical writers spoke of the human spirit, as they many times did, what did they mean by it? And how does the modern understanding coordinate with the biblical view?

We must not expect to find in the Bible a single, sharply defined concept of the human spirit. Its writers had other interests. Yet some general indications are discernible.

Four terms are used in the Bible repeatedly which are almost if not quite identical.[3] They are soul (*nephesh*, He-

[3] Arnold B. Come in *Human Spirit and Holy Spirit* (Philadelphia: Westminster Press, 1959), chapters V and VI, discusses these terms at much greater length. Though I am indebted to his presentation, I am not convinced that the fine distinctions he makes can properly be drawn from the biblical use of the terms.

brew), heart (*lebh*, Hebrew), mind (*nous*, Greek) and spirit (*ruach* in Hebrew, *pneuma* in Greek). The first of these, we noted, could be used of animal life, yet in the Bible it almost never is. It means man in all his manifold relationships —a living body but much more than body. The heart is the center, not only of desire, aspiration, and other emotions, but of conscious, purposeful activity. Solomon's prayer, "Give therefore thy servant an understanding heart to judge thy people" (I Kings 3:9 KJV), epitomizes its meanings, though the near-identity of terms is indicated by the fact that the Revised Standard Version translates it "an understanding mind." The term "mind," used somewhat less frequently than the other three, is not limited to the intellectual or cognitive activities of the self, but means the whole man as a knowing, judging, willing, acting person. The three terms meet in Jesus' rendering, according to Matthew, of the Old Testament Shema as the first and great commandment, "You shall love the Lord your God with all your heart, and with all your soul, and with all your mind" (Matt. 22:37).

But what of spirit? In many of the passages in which it is used, it seems simply to sum up and repeat what is implied in these other terms. In this context it has much the same meaning we now attach to it. That is, it connotes that aspect of the total human self whereby one thinks, feels, and wills; aspires toward high goals and at times defects from them; feels the imperatives of conscience and the joys and sorrows of human existence. In this setting it connotes what in contemporary terminology is often called the capacity of the human spirit for self-transcendence.

Yet this is not the only meaning of spirit. We have noted

that *ruach* can be used either of God's Spirit or the human spirit, and that Paul in contrasting flesh and spirit spoke of the Spirit as victorious over the impulses of the flesh. This is consistent with what the Bible indicates repeatedly, namely, that the human spirit can be radically changed as the Spirit of God in Christ acts with and upon it.

So great may be this change that we are apt to speak of "a new spirit" in a person. Actually, it is the same spirit —the same selfhood—with a radical reorientation in the direction of a new motivation, illumination, and strengthening. If the seed or ground or potentiality of such reorientation were not present in the depths of one's being, ready to respond when the Holy Spirit breaks through the incrustations of self-centeredness, the reorientation would not take place.

This is very important for two reasons. First, as has been indicated, the potentiality for the Holy Spirit's transformation of the human spirit is present because of the image of God in every man. Mar it as we will by a subtle self-centeredness or more overt forms of sin, it remains in the very nature of personhood. It is not only the mark of our kinship with God but God's channel of communication with us. Its most basic notes are found in man's capacity for worship and for moral obedience in love, and these are the major human experiences through which the Holy Spirit speaks.

Second, the term "spiritual," which is often used too narrowly to connote devotional practices or special expressions of Christian piety, gets its true meaning from the conscious relating of the human spirit to the divine Spirit in the whole life. The spiritual person, however limited in his native capacities, has a God-given wisdom which is insight rather than "smartness." To the measure in which he has "the fruit of the Spirit" it comes from God, but it comes to the person who seeks it with earnest determination. This seems to be what Paul meant when he wrote, "The unspiritual man does not receive the gifts of the Spirit of God, for they are folly to him, and he is not able to understand them because they are spiritually discerned" (I Cor. 2:14).

I shall attempt no extensive analysis of contemporary thought on the nature of the human spirit, which would carry us far beyond the legitimate boundaries of this book. Yet it should be pointed out that the best insights of modern psychology, proceeding as they do from very different foundations, corroborate at important points the biblical point of view in regard to the human spirit. Not all forms of psychology do this, but the trend appears to be in this direction.

We should not expect to find any exact correlation. So long as psychology remains within scientific bounds it does not attempt to say anything about the image of God in man, or man's destiny beyond death, or the work of the Holy Spirit. These elements are outside the sphere of empirical science and we should not expect it to deal in religious concepts or terminology. Nevertheless, within its own terrain there are significant points of convergence.

Modern thought, for the most part, agrees with the biblical view that there is no sharp dichotomy between body and spirit. Many pages of many books have been written in the past to present the opposing claims of psychophysical parallelism, interaction, a naturalism that makes the body everything and mind or spirit simply a mode of the body's functioning and, in turn, a self-psychology which regards the body mainly as the instrument of spirit for its higher ends and at times also an obstruction to their achievement. None of these is now the dominant note in modern psychology, where the emphasis is upon the unity of personality within which there are complex and variant modes of expression. In depth psychology much has been learned as to the power of unconscious impulses, neither wholly bodily nor psychic but discoverable in the experience of the total self, which lie at the root of man's behavior.

Within this unity of the total person, a significant place is being accorded to the emotional and evaluational aspects of human existence. Not only conditionings but motivations matter. What one loves and lives for goes far toward determining the nature of one's personality. In contemporary psychotherapy, the need to direct attention not only inward to understand the root of one's troubles but outward in concern for others is receiving a degree of attention which might formerly have been scoffed at as sheer sentimentality.

A generation ago a naturalistic form of behaviorism was in the ascendancy. Man was simply a complex form of animal life. His "spirit," if any, was the action of his brain cells, nervous system, and glands in reaction to the conditions set by his heredity and his environment, past and present. This point of view has not wholly disappeared and, as was indicated earlier, it left behind it the legacy of a deterministic view of human behavior. If determinism is used judiciously for the tracing and correcting of the causes of personal or social ills, it can be an important contribution to human good. When it is made to cover everything, the person becomes a piece of mechanism to be worked, and responsible selfhood goes out the window.

The depth psychology of today is realistic but less deterministic. In general, it affirms man's freedom within limits to choose his course of action and thus makes a place for moral responsibility. This is particularly true of logotherapy, or the quest for meaning. Stemming primarily from the influence of the Viennese psychologist Viktor Frankl, it is one of the most significant contemporary developments in this field.[4]

If depth psychology does not use the word sin, as it usually does not, it nevertheless recognizes in the human ego a persistent and deep-laid self-centeredness which gives rise both to antisocial behavior and to personal unhappiness. Yet on the affirmative side, it recognizes great and often hidden capacities for self-giving. Its therapy points to the value of transcendent goals beyond one's self and the need both to be loved and to love. On these grounds, the former gap between scientific psychotherapy and Christian counseling has narrowed considerably in our time.

3. HOW DOES THE HOLY SPIRIT SPEAK?

We are ready now to try to answer the question, "How may we know when it is the Holy Spirit who speaks, and not our own subsconscious impulses?"

Let us be aware that there is no infallible, inflexible answer to this question. The possibility of error is involved in the very fact of man's finiteness. The tendency to believe what one wants to believe and to find justification for what one wants to do is one of the most persistent factors in the

[4] See his *From Death-Camp to Existentialism*, now revised and enlarged as *Man's Search for Meaning: An Introduction to Logotherapy*, trans. Ilse Lasch (Boston: Beacon Press, 1962). The Christian connotations of this point of view have been admirably developed by Robert C. Leslie in *Jesus and Logotherapy* (Nashville: Abingdon Press, 1965).

subconscious ego of every man. Then, if one is a religious person, what is more natural than to claim support in the will of God? And if one is a Christian, why not assume that any strong impulsion is the voice of the Holy Spirit?

There is no absolute protection, but there are safeguards.

The first and the indispensable safeguard is what Paul called *"the mind of Christ."* This, we have seen, does not mean the ideology of Jesus in any restricted sense. It means the totality of the revelation of God in Jesus as this is discernible in his message, his ministry, his death and resurrection. Granted that the Bible leaves gaps and that the Gospels differ in some details, nevertheless the picture is clear enough so that we need be left in no doubt as to the main tenor of his message or the main notes in both his person and his work.

It is often said that the difference between the environment and times of Jesus and those of today make it impossible to find ethical guidance in the Gospels. If his words as there recorded are taken as legalistic prescriptions, this is true. If they are taken as indices of the nature and will of God, it is not true. What is universal and eternal in the revelation of God in Jesus must be appropriated and applied within the changing conditions of every age, but this does not invalidate its truth or relevance.

The basic meaning of the Christian Trinity in experience is that the leading of the Holy Spirit is the voice and will of the Father as this has been made known to us through the Son. It is apprehended through faith and lived out in love. Anything assumed to be the leading of the Holy Spirit which prompts persons to unloving words or acts, to self-righteousness, or to other forms of unholy self-centeredness which sometimes appear even in regard to holy things, must be repudiated as contrary to the Spirit of Christ. On the other hand, the more we live with Jesus as he comes to us through the New Testament and in daily companionship with the living Christ, the more clearly and potently the Spirit moves us to faith and love, and points the way to right decisions.

A second directive is suggested by the account of the coming of the Spirit at Pentecost. It came to the first Christians when they were in a receptive mood, waiting for it, and it had the effect of prompting them to share not only their prayers and praise but their daily bread. And it came, not to each in isolation, but in fellowship.

This points to *the Church*, when it is fulfilling its God-given functions, as a major channel through which the Holy Spirit speaks. The Church makes mistakes, for it is made up of fallible human men and women. Yet the Church exists for the worship of God, for the cultivation of Christian experience and Christian living, and for sharing in Christian fellowship. We have noted that it is man's capacity for worship and for moral obedience in love that are the most distinctive marks of the image of God in every man. When these are made vital and central in the human spirit through the agency of the Church, the Spirit has a channel through which to speak with marvelous power.

A third channel was intimated in the mention of *Christian fellowship*. Whether in the fellowship of worship, or of study, or of service in the name of Christ, the Holy Spirit finds an opening. This may take the form of a wise word by a Christian counselor, of prayer together about an individual's special problem, of corporate listening for light on a shared concern with the willingness to act on the light that comes. The Spirit can speak through a friendly greeting to someone lonely and afraid, and thus communicate the awareness that someone cares. He finds manifold ways to work through dedicated human selves.

One would, of course, not wish to omit the importance of *personal prayer*. It is likely that most of the readers of this book have had times when they felt sure that God was speaking to them in some great service of worship, or through the voice of a modern prophet, or in some soul-stirring personal experience. Then they have tried to pray, and nothing seemed to happen. There is not space here to repeat what I have elsewhere said at greater length.[5] It is perhaps enough to say that insofar as the barriers are of our own making, we ought to remove them instead of giving up; insofar as they are not, we can know by faith in Christ that God is with us even when the light is dim. In this assurance we can "rest in the Lord, and wait patiently for him."

Human minds are God's instruments. There is a tendency among many persons to think that the Spirit speaks only through the emotions, or through intuitive "hunches." If a strong feeling comes over one, that is God's voice or guiding hand; if one thinks the matter through calmly and tries to survey the subject from every angle including the probable consequences of a course of action, that is one's own reason. I believe it is unwarranted to draw so sharp a distinction. God speaks through the subconscious, in which the guidance seems to come intuitively; he speaks also through giving

[5] With respect to the general aspects of prayer in *Prayer and the Common Life* (Nashville: Abingdon Press, 1948); about the particular hindrances to prayer in depression and nervous turmoil in *The Dark Night of the Soul* (Nashville: Abingdon Press, 1945).

clear minds and aiding in the best thinking one can do. Neither procedure is to be disparaged, but of the two the second is likely to be the more trustworthy.

Let us be clear at this point. It is not that our own thinking is more to be trusted than divine wisdom—far from it. What is being affirmed is that God works *through our thinking,* and not alone through mysterious processes that go on beneath the level of conscious thought. The Holy Spirit may indeed speak through the latter, but not as an excuse for laziness. Our best guidance comes through a conjunction of earnest prayer, careful thought, and a sincere willingness to follow the implications of that guidance when it comes.

There is no single human pattern to follow, and no procedure that will guarantee perfect results. Yet one requirement is indispensable. Everything comes to a focus in *the willingness to act,* as far as one sees the way before him, in the Spirit of Christ. Jesus was declaring his own authority to speak as one sent by the Father when he said, "If any man's will is to do his will, he shall know whether the teaching is from God . . ." (John 7:17). Nevertheless, the word is equally relevant to us in our time and place. God will teach us much if we are responsive to his voice and willing to serve him in obedient love. If we are not, it is too likely to happen that all we hear will be the clamor of the human ego mixed with the raucous or soothing voices of the society around us.

The conclusion we come to, then, is that openness, sensitivity to God and human need, earnest search for the will of God and obedience when we find it, are indispensable to the human spirit if the Holy Spirit is to find entrance. He comes in no single mode of disclosure but in "guidance, comfort, and strength" to the total self. It is not beyond possibility that his voice be heard in the "earthquake, wind, and fire" of our current existence. It is likely that even in this setting the clarifying and strengthening note will best be heard through the still, small voice, for ears not attuned to it there may fail to hear it elsewhere.

Interwoven with all of these channels of personal illumination is the movement of the Holy Spirit in human events. Ours is a God of history, and history is in the making. At this we shall look in the next chapter.

IX

THE HOLY SPIRIT
AND
CONTROVERSIAL ISSUES

This chapter is designed as a transition from the biblical and theological issues central to the earlier ones to the practical aspects of life in the Spirit. We shall not leave behind either the Bible or theology. To do so would be to undercut one of the author's firmest convictions; namely, that both the Bible and theology are relevant to, and need to be applied in, the daily demands of Christian living.

The reference in the title to controversial issues should not be taken to mean that any definitive statement on these issues is intended. On the contrary, the chapter has two main objectives. The first is to state and give reasons for the author's position on some matters relating to the Holy Spirit on which Christians disagree. The latter part of the chapter has a somewhat different focus, for it aims to present an example—call it a case study if you will—of how the Holy Spirit can aid the conscientious and responsive Christian in making ethical decisions in a controversial situation.

166

1. SPEAKING IN TONGUES

A question which has been asked me repeatedly when I remarked in conversation that I was writing a book on the Holy Spirit is, "Do you intend to deal with the phenomenon of speaking in tongues?" The question suggests that to many minds the ancient but now revived practice of glossolalia, or of talking gibberish in a kind of religious ecstasy, is a special manifestation of the Holy Spirit. I have omitted it except for a few references in the historical context because I do not believe that it is, or ever was, any special evidence of being "filled with the Spirit."

Unquestionably, there was such a phenomenon in the early Church. Paul deals with it at length, with patience but with less than full commendation, in First Corinthians 12–14. Whether it occurred at Pentecost is a matter on which there is no general agreement. The story as we have it suggests miraculous skills in foreign languages, but perhaps an earlier version told of ecstatic utterance, which would account for the bystanders' charging the group with drunkenness. In any case, the main point of the story of Pentecost is a great new influx of spiritual power with which came a shared understanding of the gospel of Christ. To claim Pentecost as authorization for the present practice of speaking in tongues breaks down at two points: it is not a foreign language that is uttered and, as Paul took care to point out, it obscures rather than furthers understanding of the gospel.

I do not disparage religious raptures and ecstasies, even though my own temperament does not move in that direction. Certainly, a Christian ought to experience joy in his faith, and most of us are too inhibited in our expression of that joy. Yet there are ways, and other ways, of releasing inhibitions, and I do not consider the speaking with tongues to be among the most fruitful of them. In terms of the tests previously mentioned—"the mind of Christ," the fellowship of the Christian community, worship and service in love, personal prayer, earnest thought in openness to God's leading, dedicated willingness to obey the call of God when it is heard—there is no guarantee that the speaking in tongues will accompany them. It may, or it may not. These procedures and qualities of life are found at least as often among those who do not speak in tongues as among those who do. The fruit of the Spirit is love, joy, peace, patience, kindness, goodness, faithfulness, gentleness, self-control, and we are told in words that can hardly be taken lightly, "Thus you will know them by their fruits."

2. THE SACRAMENTS

At almost the opposite extreme, though at some points the extremes appear to meet, is the question of the place of the sacraments as the unique channel of the Spirit's outpouring of grace. Here the question is not whether the sacraments *are* a means of grace and vehicle of the Spirit—few Christians would doubt this—but whether they are so in any exclusive sense.

At this point I shall doubtless speak in terms of my heritage, which is Methodist, and back of that, Quaker. One of my prized possessions is a time-stained but fully legible dismissal paper by which my Quaker great-grandfather who was obdurate enough to "marry out of the meeting" and then to refuse to "make satisfaction to the meeting" by saying he was sorry he had married the girl he loved, was thereby disowned. One result of that nonconformist act of long ago is that I am a birthright Methodist, not Quaker. Yet without denying the influence of my tradition, I believe there are some other reasons for holding that the sacraments are an important, yet not all-important, channel of the Holy Spirit's work.

That this is a "sacramental universe," as William Temple declared it to be,[1] is very pertinent to this question. On the one hand, the total universe is God's world, and to the human spirit attuned to the divine Spirit, every bough and blossom, star and snowflake, expression of human love and manifestation of the quest for truth, beauty, and goodness can be the carrier of his Spirit and hence a means of grace. Yet, on the other hand, the sacraments of the Church have a special sacredness because in them the physical elements and the spiritual Presence meet to accent "the grace of the Lord Jesus Christ, the love of God and the fellowship of the Holy Spirit." While Protestants reject belief in a physical miracle of transubstantiation in the Lord's Supper, one who believes in the real presence of the Holy Spirit in the Church has no need to reject belief in the Real Presence of the living Christ in the Eucharist.

The issue comes to focus in baptism which has often been held to be the rite through which the Holy Spirit is imparted, whether in infancy or adult life. This view is supported not only by its place in the long tradition of the Church but by numerous biblical references which indicate a close con-

[1] *Nature, Man and God* (New York: Macmillan Co., 1934), chap. XIX.

junction in the early church between baptism and the receiving of the Holy Spirit (John 1:33; Acts 1:5, 8:15-17, 19:5; I Cor. 12:13; Gal. 3:27). It is related also to the fact that in all four of the Gospels the baptism of Jesus is associated with the descent of the Spirit.

That baptism is a valid sacrament—an "outward and visible sign of an inward and spiritual grace" to mark acceptance into the fellowship of Christ's followers—is hardly debatable. Questions remain as to its form and timing, but among most Christians there is little doubt of its importance. Because it means that the baptized person is now to be nurtured and sustained within the fellowship of the Christian community, not only the parents' vows in infant baptism but those of the congregation should be taken with great seriousness.

However, it is quite another matter to say that one is not a Christian unless he has been baptized, or that without this rite the Holy Spirit is not present to the Christian believer. At this point I agree not only with my Quaker ancestors but with those Christians of today who regard Christian experience as more basic than any ecclesiastical rite. That infant baptism is commonly followed by confirmation or some corresponding rite when the child is old enough to understand something of its meaning is an overt or tacit acknowledgment that baptism apart from personal experience is an incomplete channel for the Holy Spirit's ministry of grace. That both baptism and confirmation are so often forgotten or disregarded in later life is one of the most serious aspects of the secularism of our time.

3. FREE OR FORMAL WORSHIP?

Another disputed issue, related to both of the two preceding ones, is whether the Holy Spirit speaks best through formal or free forms of worship. This is almost, but not quite, identical with asking whether he speaks most vitally through traditional or through contemporary modes of expression. The answer in either case, as I see it, is that the criterion is not to be found in liturgy versus spontaneity or in time-honored diction versus contemporary speech and art forms. What matters is the degree of reverence, depth of vitality in praise and prayer, and movement toward Christ-centered living. Worship exists not for aesthetic exaltation, not for the participant's euphoria, and certainly not for the onlooker's enjoyment, but as an act of dedication of self to the glory of God. This can be done through stately liturgy or Spirit-filled exhortation, through the prayers of the ages or the speech, music, drama, or dance of today if these are sufficiently disciplined to have dignity, reverence, and fitness.

I should like to emphasize the last statement. We do not need to be Puritanical or even Victorian in regard to the use of the dance or contemporary forms of music and art in worship. Yet we do need to be discriminating. Does it have dignity, reverence, and fitness? The presentation of the Lord's Supper in jazz should not be judged by its entertainment value, its appeal to curiosity, or its novelty. Its true criterion is whether it lifts the jaded contemporary man closer into the presence of God and stirs in him a sense of the majesty and glory of the self-giving of God's Son for our salvation. So, too, with unconventional prayers. It is not their newness or their oldness, but their authenticity, that matters. Granted that there is no fixed standard of good taste or of what constitutes reverent and meaningful worship, it is essential that it be appropriate to both the nature of God and to the deeper needs of men if through it the Holy Spirit is to speak.

4. THE SPIRITUAL LIFE

Perhaps the most crucial of all disputed issues in this general area is what is meant by "the spiritual life." This phrase, so commonly used and apparently with so obvious a meaning, is by no means a clear-cut term. I have not used it much in this book because it means such different things to different people. Does it mean the inner life in contrast with the life of activity and service? If we grant, as we well may, that it should include both, how is the life within to be most fruitfully nourished? Is the practice of corporate worship sufficient? And if not, how shall we best engage in private meditation and prayer? In silence? In the reading of the Bible? In the study of the devotional classics, or of the devotional manuals of today? Is the meeting of small groups for mutual sharing and self-examination to be encouraged? Are periodic "spiritual retreats" a needed means of grace? Is the daily "quiet time" a possibility within the demands of today's world? Do we really need this time alone with God, and if so what should we expect from it?

Such questions come tumbling one upon the other. I shall not attempt to answer them here. Such procedures for the nourishing of the inner life, which means for the opening of channels for the Holy Spirit to work in us, are important. They call for time, patience, and the exercise of spiritual disciplines. Unquestionably, much good can come from any of these openings to the divine Spirit if the main end is kept in view, which is to glorify God and live a God-centered life obedient to his will. If the end is lost either in too anxious self-scrutiny or in enjoyment of one's own "spirituality," perhaps one might better be about the Father's business with less self-concern. I have never felt greatly drawn toward those forms of religious therapy which center in psychological analysis of one's shortcomings, group confession,[2] or the use of prayer as a tool for the alleviation of neuroses, though I recognize that under wise Christian leadership spiritual benefit can come out of such experiences.

The true spiritual life is responsiveness to the Holy Spirit in every aspect and concern of daily living. If we try to isolate the spiritual life into certain fragmented compartments, even though these compartments are ostensibly God-oriented, its ingrown nature becomes a source of weakness where strength ought to be. Yet, on the other hand, good moral living is not all there is of the spiritual life. The Christian's daily battle, in both small matters and great, finds engagement with two persistent questions, "What ought I to do? How can I do it?"

It is for this reason that in the remainder of the chapter I shall suggest some guidelines for decision in a contemporary controversial issue. I have selected the race question, for this is not only contemporary and controversial but widespread throughout America and the world. Any other, such as what to think and say about Vietnam, the new sex morality, or

[2] Confession of one's sin to God, to a person who has been injured with restitution where possible, and sometimes to an understanding spiritual counselor is greatly to be desired. Group confession too often runs into exhibitionism.

the John Birch Society would serve as well, but after some general guidelines we shall direct attention to this one. Let us begin with some directives from the New Testament, and primarily from the words of Paul.

5. GUIDELINES FOR DECISION [3]

(1) *Have the mind of Christ.* We have noted that in Paul's letter to the Philippians he says, "Have this mind among yourselves, which you have in Christ Jesus" (Phil. 2:5). The first requirement of Christian living is to have the mind of Christ; that is, to live with his spirit and message as they have come to us through the New Testament, through our Christian heritage, and in the stirrings of the Holy Spirit amid the conditions of our time.

(2) *Speak the truth in love.* In the letter to the Ephesians we are counseled not to be children, wavering with every new idea or form of pressure. "Rather, speaking the truth in love, we are to grow up in every way into him who is the head, into Christ" (Eph. 4:15). This puts the focus squarely where it belongs—on Christlike love and on the willingness to speak the truth, not in angry denunciation of opponents but in love.

(3) *Be aglow with the Spirit.* Putting love at the center and doing this at the leading of the Holy Spirit are brought together in a memorable capsule in Paul's letter of counsel to the church at Rome. "Let love be genuine. . . . Never flag

[3] What follows is condensed with some modifications from "The Christian in Controversy," a brochure which I wrote at the request of the Commission on Deaconess Work of the Woman's Division of Christian Service of The Methodist Church now a section of the National Division of the Board of Missions of that church. Used by permission.

in zeal, be aglow with the Spirit, serve the Lord. Rejoice in your hope, be patient in tribulation, be constant in prayer" (Rom. 12:9-12). To be constant in prayer does not mean for the most of us withdrawal to a cloister; it means living and doing our work in responsiveness to God's Spirit.

(4) *Test everything; hold fast what is good.* Again we find the directives tied together in a compact unity, for Paul writes, "Do not quench the Spirit, do not despise prophesying, but test everything; hold fast what is good, abstain from every form of evil" (I Thess. 5:19-22). This appears in the context of wise counsel about respecting authority, living peaceably, encouraging the fainthearted, being patiently helpful, doing good to one another instead of trying to get even for an injury.

(5) *All things are not expedient.* Paul wrote to the Corinthian church, "All things are lawful unto me, but all things are not expedient" (I Cor. 6:12 KJV). The Revised Standard Version renders it, "Not all things are helpful." Paul apparently was urging those to whom he wrote to have a sense of the fitness of things, to consider what would be most helpful under the circumstances, and not to let their zeal outrun their wisdom.

(6) *Do not be conformed to this world.* In a compendium of good counsel for Christians Paul writes, "Do not be conformed to this world but be transformed by the renewal of your mind, that you may prove what is the will of God, what is good and acceptable and perfect" (Rom. 12:2). The Church needs renewal; so do we all. Yet amid much talk of modes of such renewal in adaptation to the modern world, it is imperative that it should be the gospel, not the world itself, that sets the goals.

(7) *We must obey God rather than men.* Here the word is from Peter, not Paul. It was spoken during a crucial controversy in the early days of the church (Acts 5:27-42), and the climax of the story is in the apostles' continuing to do exactly what they had been forbidden to do, "rejoicing that they were counted worthy to suffer dishonor for the name" (vs. 41). Civil disobedience is not to be entered into lightly, but there are times when Christian fidelity requires it.

6. THE APPLICATION

What have these principles to do with decision in the matters of racial controversy? Obviously, not all who agree with them in church will apply them in the same way in the community. Yet if they are taken seriously, they cannot fail to make a difference, for they are basic notes in the Christian gospel. Through them the Holy Spirit speaks to our time as he did to the church in the first century. These guidelines belong together in a constellation and must be used as a unity. Yet to keep the application related to the principle, we shall review them point by point. I shall not say much about the Holy Spirit in the next few pages, but this is what the Spirit says to one Christian on this issue. Others may think differently.

About the relation of race to "the mind of Christ," there can be no question. Though apparently in the beginning of his ministry Jesus saw his mission mainly directed to his own people, the Jews, in the presence of human need he broke over all lines of racial and national division. A Syro-Phoenician woman's daughter or a Roman centurion's son was equally with a Jewish person to be loved and healed.

176

Jesus did not hesitate to talk of living water with a woman of Samaria even though at that time the Jews had no dealings with the Samaritans, and one of his greatest parables is about the compassionate act of a good Samaritan who shows true neighborliness. The early Church grasped the fact that Christ had died for all men, and everywhere the gospel was carried there was a great leveling of human distinctions, economic, racial, and social, breaking down the "middle wall of partition" (Eph. 2:14, KJV), the "dividing wall of hostility" (RSV) that tends to keep men apart.

In principle, this equality of all persons before God, regardless of race, has been generally recognized by the churches. Most of the denominations have made official declarations to this effect.

In practice, race discrimination exists widely in churches, not only in the disturbing fact that there are white churches where Negroes are not permitted to worship but in the subtle, race-oriented attitudes of thousands of church members, both South and North. What shall we do about it?

To "speak the truth in love" is the first step. It is both common sense and a basic need in any dispute to sit down together and talk things over. When the parties to the disagreement become angry and begin shouting accusations, such violence begets more violence. Speaking the truth *in love* transforms the situation. Where love is genuine, a new humility emerges on both sides and fresh insights in reaching a solution are likely to appear.

In community relations where racial tensions exist, it is important to get at the facts, for rumors and misunderstandings always cloud the issue. Where opinions differ, calm discussion is indispensable. Yet no civic organization can be expected to exercise the full reconciling power of Christian love. It is in the Church, and among committed Christians who are willing to be led by the Holy Spirit, that such love should be found in its clearest expression. If it is not, deep soul-searching and penitence are in order. It is not easy to differ profoundly on an issue yet remain friends, but by God's grace it is not impossible.

This is why it is so necessary to "be aglow with the Spirit." This, of course, does not mean some artificial radiance, or smiles where there ought to be great seriousness. When a Negro or person of another minority group is denied admission to a church or school or voting place; is refused hospital facilities, housing or employment because of his color; is told that he cannot go into a rest room, restaurant, or other places of public accommodation, it is no time for light-heartedness. Both basic justice and Christian morality require that these barriers be challenged. It is a time for action to the full limit of one's opportunity. Only the Christian who is aglow with the Spirit, fortified by prayer and a God-given assurance of the right, is likely to act, and act in the spirit of Christ.

But act how? This brings us to the next principle, to "test everything; hold fast what is good." Having ascertained the facts, what do we do?

Since the action to be taken varies with the circumstances, it is obvious that no precise formula is available. If one has some authority, either in church or community, it follows that this should be exercised with courage and justice, with both sense and sensitivity. Yet even the humblest person can speak in conversation or otherwise let his position be known, and by speaking with conviction can mold attitudes.

Where the issue comes to a vote, he can vote his convictions even if these are not on the side of the majority. Unjust restrictions become rescinded, though usually not all at once, by two great forces. One of these is a shift in public opinion, the other is the law.

These two forces are closely related. Full enforcement of the law requires not unanimous but fairly general acceptance of its rightness. This is why the molding of attitudes, to which *every person* can contribute by "standing up to be counted" is so important. However, while prejudice cannot be prohibited by law, the law can prohibit the overt effects of prejudice which result in situations of injustice. The Christian who believes that such historic political decisions as the Supreme Court decision for the desegregation of the schools in 1954, the Civil Rights Act of 1964, and the Voting Rights Act of 1965 are on the side of "liberty and justice for all" can help greatly by letting his moral support be felt in church and community.

It is at this point that the warning, "all things are not expedient," becomes both necessary and dangerous. It is necessary because otherwise we may say and do foolish things, alienating the very people we want to influence. It is dangerous because it is so easy to use it as an excuse for doing or saying nothing. To say that "the people are not ready for it" or "I must not offend the people and lose my leadership" *may* be true; it is often an alibi for lack of courage or depth of concern. If Jesus had been concerned mainly with not arousing opposition, he could have died in his bed at a ripe old age and not on a cross!

Years ago I heard a Christian leader of an earlier generation, Dr. Lyman Abbott, say something which I think can hardly be improved upon. It was, "Let courage teach you when to speak and tact teach you how." It is when these qualities are joined at the call of Christ that we have both strength and gentleness, and in this linkage lies our wisest strategy.

If we are to avoid an expediency that is mere spinelessness we must certainly not "be conformed to this world," for this world is full of racial suspicion, misunderstanding, and sheer irrational dislike. Much of this is due to the culture we live in rather than to the bad motives of other persons. Our past conditioning, often from childhood, erects the bogey of intermarriage, which is made a reason for denying any mingling in school, housing, or elsewhere. We confuse lack of opportunity with inferiority; we dislike the different. We persuade ourselves that everybody is better off if the races are kept apart. This attitude spreads to churches, and we exclude those of another race even from the house of God.

Two things are necessary. One is for those in the grip of such cultural conditioning to break loose from it by reason, experience of fellowship with those of another race, and the power of the gospel. The other is for those whose culture has not set up such barriers to understand the powerful forces that cause others to feel as they do. If both sides will do this, we can move forward together.

Our final guideline, to "obey God rather than men," must be applied in all the problems of Christian living. Only rarely does this call us to disobey the law or defy a duly constituted authority. Nevertheless, a splendid courage and deep dedication to racial justice has been shown by those Christian young people in our time who have participated in civil rights activities with the dangers incident to participation in freedom schools and voter registration. They have gone into these projects knowing that not only imprisonment but in some cases their lives were at stake, and at the cost of opposition from their parents who naturally wish them not to incur danger. Yet they have gone in serious concern and without violence to give their witness. Even those who disagree with the procedure can scarcely fail to respect the spirit that calls it forth.

In such procedures as have been indicated, it is not necessary, and usually not judicious, to talk very much about the Holy Spirit. In most controversial issues, to secure full results we must work in cooperation with others to whom the Holy Spirit is a meaningless term. Yet a deeper reason for reticence is the ever-present danger that the Holy Spirit may be appealed to as a bulwark of one's own self-formed desires and opinions. Nevertheless, if the Christian is to possess the wisdom, the courage, and the staying power to see such matters through—or as is more likely, to put in his contribution and wait for God to give the fruitage—the Holy Spirit is an immensely vital factor in his life. This, in the widest possible context, *is* the spiritual life.

X

THE HOLY SPIRIT
IN
THE LIFE OF TODAY

We have now swung full circle from the brief
reference in the introductory chapter to the Holy Spirit in
today's world through the biblical, theological, ecclesiological,
and psychological foundations of belief to the concrete problems of ethical decision in our time. It is appropriate to end
the book with a further look at the actual and potential relation of the Holy Spirit to the life of today.

Let the reader be advised that what appears in this chapter
will be a look—not a full analysis. To supply the latter would
require a book in itself, or, more accurately, many books.
What is aimed at is simply to present some evidences that
the modern world, with all its gigantic changes which often
appear chaotic and at some points demonic, is nevertheless
a sphere in which the Spirit of God is at work.

No apologies are in order for having presented at some
length a biblical and theological foundation for a recognition
if not full understanding of that Breath of God which, we are
told on high authority, is like "the wind [that] blows where it

wills, and you hear the sound of it, but you do not know whence it comes or whither it goes" (John 3:8). Yet if one's historical and theoretical understanding does not lead to a deeper sense of being "born of the Spirit," with a renewal of Pentecostal power in the individual and society, something is wrong somewhere.

We began this book with a brief allusion to the obvious fact that the Holy Spirit, in spite of being on the lips of virtually every church-going Christian, is a neglected doctrine. It is appropriate at this point to ask why. It is not primarily that the doctrine is abstract, mysterious, and therefore difficult; this is true of every Christian doctrine if one probes beyond its most immediate simplicities. The problem may lie in the fact that the human and divine elements are more closely inter-twined than in most aspects of Christian belief, and we are baffled at the point of trying to separate them. Granted that the Holy Spirit is not the human spirit and that there are ways of distinguishing them, this still does not resolve the issue. Perhaps an even more potent, though related, reason for our bafflement is that the Spirit of God is so close to us, so essential to the totality of Christian living, that it is not easy to stand off and take an objective look at it. The very able playwright and lay theologian, Dorothy Sayers, suggests this by way of the analogy of the difficulty of seeing the movement of one's own eye:

The eye is the instrument by which we see everything, and for that reason it is the one thing we cannot see with truth. The same thing is true of our Power of response to a book, or to anything else; incidentally, this is why books about the Holy Ghost are apt to be curiously difficult and unsatisfactory—we can-

183

not really look at the movement of the Spirit, just because It is the Power by which we do the looking.[1]

Nevertheless, it is the movement of the Spirit in the immediate environs of human living that matters most. If we do not discern God at work where we are, Christian doctrine is not only impoverished in its content but largely futile in its results. Therefore, what of the movement of the Spirit in the life of today?

1. THE LIFE OF TODAY

No extensive presentation of the life of today is needed, for no one will have persisted in reading this book thus far who does not know that we are living in a very complex and at many points disordered society. If we did not know it already from personal experience, every news report with its account of political, economic, and racial tension, escalating crime, juvenile and adolescent delinquency, broken homes, sexual looseness, and slipping standards on many fronts would tell us so. Death on the highways, not only on holiday weekends but throughout the year, with the drunkenness which so often precipitates it, is a gruesome symptom of our disordered times. The enormous consumption of tranquilizers is its attempted medicine. These things lie close at hand. Then over everything, here and around the world, hang three perils like the proverbial sword of Damocles—the danger of atomic destruction, the spread of world communism, and the population explosion which if uncurbed can precipitate untold misery, conflict, and death.

[1] *The Mind of the Maker* (New York: Harcourt, Brace & World, 1941), p. 115.

This picture is by no means a happy one. Nobody in obsession with his own comfort or the relative ease and security of his personal life ought to overlook it. Yet the picture is distorted unless we note also signs of progress. The advance of technology has not only ushered in the nuclear-space age and an economic revolution with the accompanying upheavals of automation, but it has produced in America the highest standard of living known to man and holds the promise of great advances among the underprivileged peoples of the earth if its fruits can be shared. We have more and better education than our fathers had. There have been great advances in the conquest of disease, and there is a better understanding, even if not curtailment, of mental illness. The "triple revolution," so-called, includes not only cybernetics and weaponry, but human rights.[2] In recent years there have been great advances in civil rights and concern for the aged. And even amid the tensions of violent revolution and at times appalling bloodshed, there has been an enlarging sense of the imperative need of world cooperation and international responsibility.

I do not propose to discuss these gigantic changes in human affairs except as they bear on the major theme of this book. There is a connection, for the social climate of our day has had its effect on trends in theology and in attitudes held toward the churches.

[2] In March, 1964, a group of thirty-two economists, labor leaders, and business and professional men, calling themselves "the Ad Hoc Committee on the Triple Revolution," prepared and sent to President Johnson a remarkably provocative and vital statement on this theme. It has been commented upon in hundreds of publications, and is reprinted in the *Information Service* of the National Council of Churches for May 22, 1965.

2. WINDS OF DOCTRINE

The theology of any age not only transmits the insights and convictions of the past but reflects the tenor of the times. It affirms whatever ground the Christian faith gives to stand on amid the shifting currents of secular thought, and at the same time it is in some measure molded by them.

We live not only in an interesting theological era, but on the whole a very encouraging one. Fundamentalism with its stress on biblical literalism is not dead, but it has definitely waned within the past fifty years and is seldom defended by the leaders of religious thought. Among its former defenders a more open-ended conservatism has largely replaced it. In the major seminaries and among theologians the liberalism of fifty years ago is now commonly castigated and disparaged. However, it has left two important if unappreciated legacies: the wide acceptance of the historical approach to the Bible and concern for the relevance of the Christian gospel to society. The rise of neo-orthodoxy, more accurately called neo-Reformation thought, under the leadership of such giants as Barth, Brunner, and the two Niebuhrs brought about a fresh restatement of notes often underestimated, though not overlooked, by the liberals. Among these were the transcendent holiness of God, the reality and depth of human sin, and the centrality of biblical theology.

Then came existentialism. In its Christian forms this was a recovery of the Kierkegaardian emphasis on "that solitary individual"; yet not wholly so for it was centered on the individual's existence within the currents and moods of a modern, science-oriented world. Its primary prophets came to be thought of as Tillich, Bultmann, and Bonhoeffer. In spite

186

of wide differences in the thought of these men they meet in the demand that Christian faith, if it is to continue to exist at all, must answer the questions and be relevant to the tenor of contemporary life.

Thus far, we seemed to be moving toward an emphasis on the great essentials of Christian faith, the emphasis varying within these theological currents but with no radical disparity that could not be synthesized in essentials. This continues to be the main stream of Christian thought.

Of late, however, a new phenomenon has arisen. It is epitomized in the Nietzschean phrase so commonly bandied about, that "God is dead."

What does this mean? It appears to be a radical surrender of theistic faith to the secularism of the modern world, either an overt atheism or such a surrender of God's objective reality and transcendence that the only God left is within man and the human scene. It is Christian relevance to the contemporary world gone to seed to the point of sheer irrelevance because it has lost its reason for existing.

There were intimations in this direction, though not the full development of its implications, in Bishop Robinson's widely discussed *Honest to God*. I believe that the Bishop inconsistently grafts together certain elements from Tillich, Bultmann, and Bonhoeffer without sufficiently taking into account the full sweep of their systems. Bonhoeffer, for example, is basically Barthian in his theology. If he could have been spared to be alive today I suspect he would be surprised to find that so much has been made of his references to "Christianity without religion" in a world "come of age," of which he spoke so briefly but graphically in his letters from prison. However, Bishop Robinson does not say there is no God.

187

He considerably qualifies if he does not repudiate the transcendence of God, but I do not find him rejecting God's existence. The book has called forth many rejoinders because it is tangent to Christian faith rather than a full statement of it, but as an index of what the modern mind finds congenial it has much significance. I find quite suggestive this statement in a review of an answer to it, *"Honest to God* emerged from a 'generating situation' as surely as any book ever did. . . . [It] is not a statement to be proved right or wrong; it is a symptom of a situation which we might not have been aware of, and which we are now spurred on to remedy." [3]

In Bishop Robinson's more recent book, *The New Reformation,* he continues, although along less disturbing lines, this emphasis on the need to serve the present age through modes of thought adapted to it. He finds the Holy Spirit at work in the present ferment. "There has been a troubling of the waters such as betokens the quickening power of the Spirit, a rustling in the tree-tops such as David was given as a sign that the Lord had passed on before him and that he must act." [4]

There are others, however, who say that God is dead. What do they mean by it? Perhaps only that God no longer functions as an important item in the beliefs and/or decisions of modern society, for secularism has triumphed. Yet to some who are teaching and writing in the field of religion it seems to mean more than that. Paul van Buren not only affirms the

[3] Erik Routley in a review of D. T. Niles' "We Know in Part" in *Religion in Life* (Summer, 1965), p. 471.
[4] *The New Reformation* (Philadelphia: Westminster Press, 1965), p. 17.

dissolution of the Absolute as a "socio-psychological fact," but gives this word of caution, "It means that religion must not only become much more guarded in speaking of God (if not give this up altogether); it means also that more care be exercised in speaking of 'unique revelation,' 'absolute commitment,' and some single 'Ultimate concern.'"[5] There are others who apparently "give this up altogether." In *The Christian Century's* series by younger but mature theologians on "How I Am Making Up My Mind," Thomas J. J. Altizer rejoices in the death of God as opening the door to the Word of faith.

Once we can accept the death of God as a final and irrevocable event, then we can open ourselves to the full actuality of our history as an epiphany of the Word of faith. . . .

The radical theologian will insist that a theology which continues even in our time to proclaim the reality of God is closed to the contemporary reality of the incarnation.[6]

What shall we make of all this? It needs to be said, in the first place, that there is nothing new in this except the verbiage. The death of God closely resembles old-fashioned humanism but in a new dress. From the time of Celsus in the late second century whom Origen felt called upon to answer, through the "cultured despisers" to whom Schleirmacher spoke in his *Addresses on Religion,* and on into the burgeon-

[5] "The Dissolution of the Absolute" in *Religion in Life* (Summer, 1965) p. 342. A similar point of view is expressed in Paul van Buren's *The Secular Meaning of the Gospel* (New York: Macmillan Co., 1963) and in William Hamilton's *The New Essence of Christianity* (New York: Association Press, 1961).

[6] *The Christian Century* (July 7, 1965), pp. 866-67.

ing humanism of the early part of this century, particularly the 1920's and early 1930's, it has all been said before though in different words. It has often caused a considerable stir and has evoked sometimes despair, sometimes heated rejoinders, but has never succeeded in killing either God or the main community of his followers, the Christian Church.

My second observation is that it has succeeded in disturbing a good many Christians, and among them that particularly vulnerable group, seminarians and young ministers. There are numerous reasons for the falling off of candidates for the ministry in these days, and for the flight of others from the parish ministry into various forms of service outside the local congregation. Secularism in the atmosphere, status-bound congregations who refuse to respond to social challenges, the irrelevance of much that goes on in churches, and plain discouragement are among these reasons. Yet in more than a few instances, it is because the seminary "winds of doctrine," legitimately blowing this way and that to encourage freedom of thought and acquaintance with the modern mood, have left the young minister with too little solid food that will either sustain his own life of faith or give him something to impart to his people. When this occurs it often seems the most honest—not simply the easiest or the most lucrative—thing to do to find some other form of service.

3. THE WINDS OF THE SPIRIT IN SOCIETY

Reference was made a moment ago to winds of doctrine. But what of the breath of the Holy Spirit? Is this blowing in the life of today?

The Holy Spirit is where God is, not only in the primordial

creativity of long ago or in those great events which gave rise to the Holy Scriptures, but throughout human history to the present. This does not mean that the presence of God has been equally manifest at all times, or that this Presence has always been called the Holy Spirit. Nevertheless, the Spirit of God is wherever God is at work, and that is everywhere even in the midst of the darkest days and the most sordid situations. He is alive even where his demise is most forcefully announced.

If we believe this, it is not presumptuous to say that God is present in the events of our time, even where he seems most hidden. This is not to say in any predestinarian sense that God ordains the world to be in the sorry state it is in. There is much about it that must sorely grieve the heart of God, both in the conflicts and perils of the outward social situation and in human attitudes of self-will and self-seeking, materialistic values, and flippancy regarding the most serious things of life. Nevertheless, God is here within his world, and within the people whom he has made in his own image. Wherever there is forward movement toward the kind of world that accords with the spirit and message of Jesus, there we may be assured that God is at work.

God is clearly present in a growing concern for the poor, the sick, and the disfranchised; in better education at all age levels and in the face of age-long racial and social barriers; in the emergence to nationhood of many new lands and the stirrings within them of the possibilities of having bread, freedom, and dignity; in long strides toward freedom and racial equality for the underprivileged in America. That many, perhaps most, of these changes have come about through the effort of persons who do not profess to speak or act in the name of God does not alter the fact that God has been using these efforts for the fulfillment of his will and the forward movement of his kingdom. Even though unacknowledged, his Spirit is present in every movement toward human good.

In the seventy-sixth Psalm we read:

Surely the wrath of men shall praise thee;
the residue of wrath thou wilt gird upon thee. (vs. 10.)

The cryptic affirmation that God makes the wrath of men to praise him has been illustrated and found to be true more than once in our time. A conspicuous example is the challenge to social justice presented by atheistic and totalitarian communism. It is, of course, not certain what would have happened without it but the chances are that this colossal gadfly has urged us forward faster than we would have been likely to move without its sting. Another example, evident to the careful observer of modern literature and especially its novels, poetry, and drama, is that beneath a frank and often near-obscene portrayal of the seamy side of modern life runs a serious note of concern for what Christian theology calls God, sin, and redemption.[7] Indeed, even the "death of God" cult can make us more aware of the reality of the living God!

It is less easy to discern the presence of the Holy Spirit

[7] To give specific illustrations would carry us too far afield for the limits of this book. Excellent studies are found in two symposiums, *Christian Faith and the Contemporary Arts*, ed. by Finley Eversole (Nashville: Abingdon Press, 1962) and *The Climate of Faith in Modern Literature*, ed. by Nathan A. Scott, Jr. (New York: Seabury Press, 1964). A valuable brief survey is given by John Killinger in an article, "The Uses of Agnosticism: Secularism in Modern Literature" which appeared in *Religion in Life* (Summer, 1965). See also his book, *The Failure of Theology in Modern Literature* (Nashville: Abingdon Press, 1963).

in the combination of unrest and superficiality which pervades our society. Shall we say that God is at work where Christian values are flouted and the Church is either ignored outright or, if it receives attention at all, is ridiculed and attacked? I do not maintain that these attitudes are expressions of the divine Spirit. Yet if they arouse us from lethargy to constructive Christian action God can use even these things to advance his purposes.

4. THE SPIRIT AT WORK IN THE CHURCHES

It is not enough, though it is crucially important, to see that the winds of the Spirit are present in the social movements and even the social crises of our day. What of the presence of the Spirit in the contemporary Church? As the community of Christ's followers, this ought to be the place where we should discern the Spirit at work with the greatest light and power. Do we? That is a very large and vital question.

It has become very customary to speak of this as a "post-Christian" era, and to decry the Church as ingrown, sold out to secularism, irrelevant to the needs of today's world. This is almost the equivalent of saying that the Holy Spirit has given up on the Church and moved out. Though it is seldom put in just this way, a considerable number of Christians, or at least of those who consider themselves Christ's followers, seem to have moved out with him.

Some of the protests against the contemporary Church stem from an honest concern to correct its defects of shallowness and irrelevancy and make of it a more vital carrier of the gospel of Christ. Yet not all do. And not all who bring charges show a loving and determined willingness either to see the good side of contemporary church life or to work within it in spite of defects to make it better. It is significant that relatively few of those who say most about the irrelevancy of the Church are parish ministers. The major part of the outcry comes either from those in some form of detached Christian service or from those whose primary interest in social action overshadows their sensitivity to other constructive notes within the life of the Church.

If one is close enough to the Church to view it both sympathetically and critically, what does he see? Naturally, not all see it in just the same way, for both churches and individuals have a "personal equation." Yet would not the picture be somewhat like this?

First, there is ground for tremendous rejoicing in the ecumenical movement, and in particular for the growth of understanding and fellowship between Roman Catholics and Protestants. While it was the missionary movement that Archbishop Temple called "the great new fact of our time," the misquotation which has applied these words times without number to the ecumenical movement within Protestantism and Eastern Orthodoxy is justified by the facts if not by the footnotes. In his enthronement address as Archbishop of Canterbury, speaking of the worldwide outreach of the missionary enterprise and its humanly unplanned but God-given fruitage he said, "Almost incidentally the great world-fellowship has arisen; it is the great new fact of our era." [8] His own contributions to the ecumenical movement, cut short by his too early death, plus those of many others fully exem-

[8] In *The Church Looks Forward* (New York: Macmillan Co., 1944), p. 2.

plify the application of these words to a great world fellowship of churches as well as of individual Christians. Then, by an amazing outpouring of the Holy Spirit through his servant Pope John XXIII in the *aggiornamento* that has been carried forward through the Second Vatican Council and many acts of spiritual fellowship at the local level, the barriers that long kept Catholic and Protestant apart have been rapidly coming down. Who can say that this is not the work of the Holy Spirit in the churches?

This same missionary movement goes forward, not unimpeded, but with great courage, dedication, and wisdom in the midst of political obstacles and the rising tide of nationalism in what was formerly viewed as mission territory. In the emergence of strong indigenous Christian leadership in many lands, in diversified services along many lines to meet human needs, and in the determined survival of Christian loyalties and indigenous churches under Communist domination, there is again a significant witness to the Holy Spirit as "God present with us for guidance, for comfort, and for strength." That there has been some silencing of the churches under political domination was wholly to be expected; the miracle attesting the Spirit's power and presence is that these churches still speak at all.

Within the American scene I have been watching the currents of church life now for a good many years. Without claiming any superior wisdom it may perhaps be said that this span of years affords a perspective not so readily available to younger observers. Within it the outcry of the irrelevancy of the churches with desertion for other pastures has become a familiar sound. It was louder than usual in the years following World War I, as it is today, but it has never been absent.

Nevertheless, within this same period there have been numerous creative developments of great importance.

As I see it, the movement in the churches over the past fifty years has been predominantly forward. I have already spoken of three great forward movements: a better theology, closer to both the mainstream of Christian belief and to the human situation; the ecumenical movement in its many ramifications; and the trend in missions toward a more diversified service in partnership with indigenous leadership. To these must be added a recovery, which is far more than a restatement, of the Reformation emphasis on the priesthood of all believers. Within both Protestant and Roman Catholic circles much fresh attention is being given to the mission and calling of the laity, enmeshed within the secularism of the modern world, to be the Church within the manifold relationships of daily life and thus to serve as a transforming leaven in society.

To these outstanding developments must be added others which I must enumerate only briefly. We have better Christian education for all ages, including adults as well as children and youth; a growing interest in lay theology and wider understanding among laymen not only of the basic affirmations of Christian faith but of its relevance to life; among many thousands of college-trained Christian laymen a better knowledge of the Bible and related fields through the courses now offered in the curriculums of many colleges and universities; a better trained ministry, with the requirement of adequate seminary training for the minister greatly increased over former days; less noisy and clamorous but more reverent public worship; a better understanding of pastoral counseling; more attention directed to the importance of

Christian family life, not in regard to the family altar only which has declined in the hurry of modern life but to the total climate of the Christian home.

To these long-range movements have been added in recent years numerous new developments in the renewal of the Church. Among them, along with the new emphasis on the laity as the Church within the world, are to be found the formation of lay academies and institutes in many centers; the meeting of small groups of concerned Christians for discussion, study, worship, and a more close-knit fellowship; numerous projects aimed at a closer connection between religion and the arts; institutional and industrial chaplaincies; new forms of ministry to students in the universities; and varied forms of outreach through coffee houses and other centers for fellowship to try to reach the lonely and "off-beat" members of society through Christian understanding and acceptance.

The charge most often brought against the churches is their hesitancy at the point of the struggle for social justice and slowness in achieving racial integration. There is truth in these charges but they are not wholly true. There have been great strides toward the elimination of segregation in recent years, and this applies to churches as well as to other social structures. Not only has the Commission on Religion and Race of the National Council of Churches been remarkably active, but in thousands of local churches doors have been opened and courageous utterances in behalf of racial justice have been spoken. This is probably more significant than the virtually unanimous affirmations of racial equality by the governing bodies of denominations. The clergy outstrip the laity in their concern over great social issues, yet the

197

recent and growing accent on the importance of the laity as the Church within the world has not gone unheeded. Particularly in the field of civil rights and racial justice, young Christians in the midst of a formerly apathetic generation have found a cause to which they can give themselves with great devotion, while their elders move somewhat more cautiously toward throwing their weight on the side of equality and justice.

To revert to the matter of theology at the congregational level, we find something of a paradox. Among theologians, theological liberalism tends to be stigmatized as a relic of the nineteenth century, while social liberalism is espoused. At the local level, almost the opposite is the case. Among the people, there is less of biblical literalism, less alarm at the historical approach to the Bible as it is at last seeping down from the seminaries, less dogmatism of an unchristian nature in both pulpit and pew. Ministers with a strong social conscience are often still under fire, but heresy trials are virtually a thing of the past.

Added to these overt movements within the churches is a more intangible factor which is too often overlooked, if not disparaged, by the critics. This is the pervasive force of the Church's spiritual ministry. It is true that secularism is widely prevalent in our churches, and that what it means to be a true follower of Christ rather than simply a decent and respectable citizen is too often unrecognized. Yet the other side of this situation is the fact that there are millions of Christians, in America and around the world, to whom the Church means a great deal. If its spiritual ministrations were to be removed they would be greatly missed.

Such persons make church attendance the habitual pattern of their lives. They contribute money and effort to the support of their churches. They seek its ministry especially in the high and low moments of life such as marriage, family crises, sickness, and death, but they do not limit their connections to these periods. In ways of which they may not be fully conscious and which it is not easy to pin down concretely, they carry their religion into life. Most of them do not talk much about it. Relatively few would be able to articulate just what Christ and his Church means to them. Yet without the Church as the carrier and embodiment of their religion, life would be quite different for them.

These are the great body of the substantial lay members of our churches. Among them are more than a few unheralded Christian saints. As long as any considerable number of persons like this remain, this is not a post-Christian era.

If what has been stated in the preceding paragraphs is a true description, no one can view these facts objectively and doubt that the Holy Spirit has been powerfully at work in the churches. This is by no means to say that everything is as it should be. I could give my list of the shortcomings of both churches and church members, and have done so in other connections. I think I know as well as anybody that there is serious injustice, ill will, suffering, and sin in the modern world, and that the churches have not been as active as they should have been in their high responsibility as carriers of the gospel of Christ and channels of the Holy Spirit. Yet I also believe that the winds of the Spirit have been blowing mightily in such matters as have been mentioned, and that because of them we should rejoice and take courage.

Here I must leave the matter. Perhaps my concluding word,

in a day of anxiety and uncertainty, may well be lifted from Paul's letter to the Romans, "May the God of hope fill you with all joy and peace in believing, so that by the power of the Holy Spirit you may abound in hope" (Rom. 15:13). And may the fellowship of the Holy Spirit be with us all.

INDEX